Lionel Heinic

Wonderful
FRENCH RIVIERA
Coastline and Country

Photographs: Hervé Champollion
Translated by: Angela Moyon

ÉDITIONS OUEST-FRANCE
13, rue du Breil, Rennes

Grasse: the world's perfume capital!

Saint-Raphaël: Europe's Copacabana (minus the samba !).

The Romans left their mark on the Cimiez District of Nice.

A "palette of colours"
waiting to be discovered : Riviera and Var

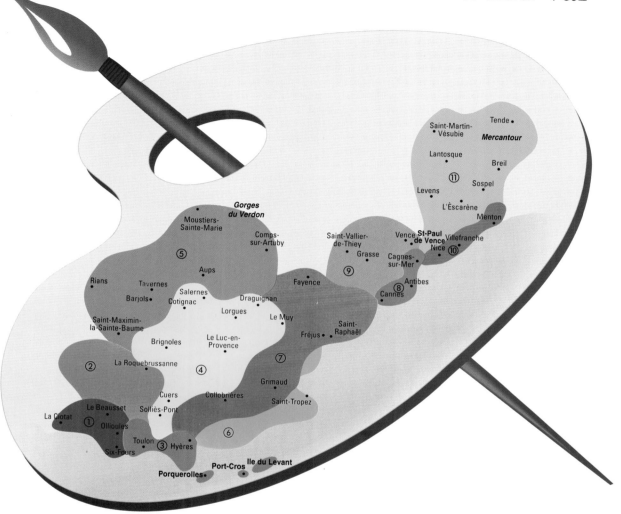

The creeks along the Golden Coast Road:
a succession of azure blue water flanked by red porphyry...

The charterhouse at La Verne.
It is built of serpentine, a green stone with strange reflections...

RIVIERA, VAR
AND "PACA" REGION

Among the twenty-two "regions" forming the administrative subdivisions of France, the one known as "PACA" (which is indubitably the most beautiful of them all) includes six *départements* viz. *Bouches-du-Rhône, Vaucluse, Alpes-de-Haute-Provence, Hautes-Alpes, Var* and *Alpes-Maritimes. Hautes-Alpes* has been set aside for it has greater affinities with the Dauphiny area than with Provence. The first three *départements* on the list have already been described in an earlier work (*Wonderful Provence*, a recent publication).

This left *Var* and *Alpes-Maritimes* and it is these *départements* which have been brought together here under the title *French Riviera, Coastline and Country.*

Although the book deals with a "specific" subject, it covers a mosaic of very different areas, a truth which becomes evident in the many, and varied, "localities" that go to make up Provence. Indeed, Provence is an area of many faces and the plural would be more appropriate than the singular. The part of the PACA region formed by the two *départements* described in this book bears this out.

How can any one work deal with an area such as the coastline of Var and a hinterland that stretches as far as the Verdon Gorge on the one hand and, on the other, the Riviera itself with beauty spots as different as the Gulf of Saint-Tropez, the Golden Coast Road (*Corniche d'Or*), the bay at Cannes and Cap d'Antibes, or the Promenade des Anglais? Not to mention Nice and its carnival, Menton and its orange trees, and a Riviera that is an introduction (though it remains resolutely separate!) to Italy, just a few miles down the road. Added to this, there is the even stranger character of a mountain-ous hinterland (a land ermine-white and azure-blue) produced by Nature, set scarcely more than an hour's drive from the coast and forming a world that, to say the least, is totally un-expected!

Being well aware of this diversity, we have been careful to divide the title of this book into "Coastline and Country" but, having said this, it remains to be seen whether this is an effective distinction. It is up to the reader to decide as he turns over the pages, going from one surprise to another, the only proof of true discovery.

GLIMPSES OF THE COTE D'AZUR AND THE VAR AREA

Port-Cros.

The harbour in Bandol.

Glazed earthenware from Moustiers (photo by Bruno Servel).

The beaches: Some people consider that the *Côte d'Azur* belongs, to all intents and purposes, to Alpes-Maritimes, while others defend the point of view that the *Côte* begins beyond Toulon, an option which includes most of the coastline of Var where the amenities often bear comparison with those provided in the more famous resorts in the extreme south-eastern corner of France. There are the grandiose boulders in *Le Brusc* (within the town, in Var, of *Six-Fours*), and the splendid red porphyry creeks that delight the eye along the famous *Gold Road* from Saint-Raphaël to Cannes! The sights are definitely different but the aesthetic emotion remains the same. The same applies to the beaches, whether they are long stretches of fine sand between sea and pinewood, the isthmus of *La Capte* (near *Hyères*) or the "elegant" beaches of *Cannes, Juan* or *La Garoupe*, all of them as popular as their colleagues in Saint-Tropez - *Pampelonne* and *Bora-Bora*.
So, who wins the victor's palms? The palm trees, of course, for they are to be seen everywhere, from the western tip of Var to the Italian border!

Sea angling, yachting and water sports: Again for the same reason relating to the length of their respective coastlines, the two *départements* described in this book have much to offer as regards the sea. Angling, of course, with fish being more qualitative than quantitative, but also yachting, whose success has led to the creation of a plethora of harbours and marinas providing anchorage for fine sailing boats and for powerful speed boats or luxury yachts.
Then come water sports which by no means lag behind the others! Apart from the various races, regattas etc. there is water skiing and, of course, windsurfing, with boards that fly across the waves, moved by the force of the wind or the sea... And who could forget the tranquil pedal boats, the traditional complement to the sunshade and suntan oil. Why not, indeed, mention minority sports such as parascending?

Crafts: First and foremost among the craft activities is, of course, pottery and everything related to it and although Moustiers-Sainte Marie lies within the *département* of Alpes-de-Haute-Provence, it is so close to Var that it is a natural part of it, situated as it is within the Verdon Gorge area, and we may perhaps be granted literary licence if we carry over from one bank of the tumbling river to the other (taking all necessary precautions) a few precious piles of plates.
There is no such problem for Vallauris. It belongs to the *département* of Alpes-Maritime, a fact that is as undeniable as was the strong influence of *Picasso* leading to the expansion of the craft of pottery within this small town. While on the subject of crafts, though, we must mention the thousand and one objects made from materials as diverse as wood (mainly olive), fabrics (wool, silk, linen, cotton etc.), leather, herbs, dried flowers, precious stones, wrought iron, gold, silver, copper ... and glass (Biot).

Museums and Exhibitions: In the two *départements* covered in this book, there are countless museums. Some have the traditional structure (paintings, sculptures, precious books, gold and silverware etc.); others have more unusual contents. Take, for example, the **Allied Landings Museum** (August 44 in Provence) on *Mont Faron* in Toulon, or the **Culinary Arts Museum** (Escoffier) in Villeneuve-Loubet, or the **Oceanography Museum** in Monaco...

However, if we stay with the more usual type of museum, we can list the following, chosen at random: **International Art Exhibition** (Toulon), **Fragonard Museum** (Grasse), **Jean Cocteau Museum** (Menton), **International Naive Art Museum** (Nice), **National Marc Chagall Biblical Art Museum** (Nice), **Matisse Museum** (Nice), **Raoul Dufy Gallery-Museum** (Nice), **Picasso Castle Museum** (Vallauris), **Picasso Museum** (Antibes - 220 works!), **National Fernand Léger Museum** (Biot), **Modern Art Museum** in the Castle in Les Hauts-de-Cagnes (Cagnes-sur-Mer), **Renoir Museum** (Les Hauts-de-Cagnes) and, last but by no means least, the prestigious **Maeght Foundation** (Saint-Paul-de-Vence).

The Maeght Foundation.

Hunting, shooting and fishing: As far as hunting and freshwater fishing are concerned, the two *départements* are better than average. The 150 clubs in Var have a membership of 27,000 hunters, while in Alpes-Maritimes there are 12,000 licence-holders in the same number of clubs. There is plenty of game in Var, especially thrushes. In Alpes-Maritimes, where partridge is in abundant supply, we have to distinguish between the coastal area and the hinterland (medium and high altitudes) where you will find those who specialise in hunting larger game (deer and, although this is subject to stringent regulations, moufflon and chamois). As for wild boar, they are subject to fewer regulations.

Turning to angling, Var (24 clubs, 15,000 members) has a large number of rivers and extensive lakes (*Sainte-Croix, Quinson, Gréoux, Saint-Cassien*). Fish to be found here include trout, pike, char, pike perch, sheat-fish, and (in Saint-Cassien) carp. In Alpes-Maritimes, the 11,000 members of twenty angling clubs can enjoy their favourite pastime in the many rivers and mountain streams running down from the mountaintop and high valleys of the hinterland.

Lake Carcès.

Wine: Because of the extensive nature of its vineyards, Var ranks high on the list of wine-producing *départements*. It includes almost the entire area granted the *Côtes de Provence* appellation although, here and there, this one gives way to various other appellations, covering much smaller areas but nevertheless producing quality wines. Among them are the *Coteaux Varois, Coteaux d'Aix*, or the aristocratic *Bandol* produced in eight towns or villages, all of them within Var.

Beyond the vineyards, it is horticulture that takes pride of place (there are a large number of horticulturalists in Var). This, though, does not prevent Alpes-Maritimes from producing excellent wines such as *Côtes de Bellet* in *Villars-sur-Var, Coteaux de la Gaude* etc.

The vineyards at Pierrefeu-du-Var.

The traditional ingredients of bouillabaisse (photo by Claude Herlédan).

Local food: As far as good food is concerned, it is the great Provençal recipes that are used throughout the region although each small area has its own special recipes based on local produce (the famous "early vegetables"). There are, for example, the inimitable *artichokes à la Barigoule*, the mouthwatering *asparagus* or *courgette batter puddings*, and the *stuffed cabbage leaves "sou façoun"* served in the Grasse area.

The cuisine of Nice has a place apart for it has its own catalogue of good food, showing its ability (and this is particularly praiseworthy) to be sufficiently different from its Italian neighbour to compete with it. There is, of course, pasta and seafood but there are also herbs and spices.

A folk festival in Allauch.

Special events and folk festivals: Traditional festivals are survivors of religious ritual, and many of them take on a very particular form. As to the Fairs, they are not only important for the local economy; they are also enjoyable entertainment. Here and there, you will find music or drama festivals which have become increasingly fashionable over the years.

As regards the *traditional* festivals (although the **Jazz Festival** in Antibes/Juan-les-Pins or the **Film Festival** in Cannes have become traditional with the passage of time), there is the superb *Flower Festival* in **Bormes-les-Mimosas** in June, and the famous *Bravade* in Saint-Tropez on 15th June when musket fire recalls the warring skills of the locals in days gone by. But there is no doubt that the best of all the traditional festivities is the *Nice Carnival* which begins ten days before Pancake Tuesday. It includes a whole succession of parades with floats, caricatures of famous people, battles of flowers or confetti, fireworks displays, dances etc. At the same time **Menton** begins its splendid *Lemon Festival*.

The Frégate Golf Course.

Golf: All over the world, this sport is enjoying a prodigious upsurge of popularity and the same applies to our two *départements*, Var and Alpes-Maritimes. In Var, there are a dozen courses, some well known to several generations of golfers, others like the *Golf de Frégate* in **Bandol/Saint-Cyr** (cf. photo opposite) developed, as is commonplace at the present time, at the same time as the hotel complexes, around wine-growing estates. Among the "traditional" courses, let us just mention, *Gassin, Grimaud/Beauvallon, Les Issambres/Sainte-Maxime, La Motte, Roquebrune-sur-Argens, Saint Raphaël/Estérel, Valescure* (of course!), *Agay, Brigoles* and *La Londe-des-Maures*.

There are almost twice as many in Alpes-Maritimes, including *Cannes/Mandelieu, Monaco/Mont-Agel, Valbonne/Sophia Antipolis, Biot, Le Cannet, Opio, Gréolières, Mougins, Tende,* and *Spéracédès*.

Markets: It was Gilbert Bécaud who sang of the "*Markets of Provence*", and they are sure to delight you. Every village has its own market day(s) so make the best of them for this is a golden opportunity to discover not only the dazzling array of colours and the incomparable scents of the products of Provence but also the flavour of the language that goes with them!

The market on Cours Lafayette in Toulon.

Pétanque: The game was first played in *La Ciotat*, where the *cinema industry* was born thanks to the *Lumière* brothers. This may explain the extent to which those indulging in the game tend to "play to the gallery" in an effort to distract the other players. In this respect, it is no exaggeration to say that this very popular game is, first and foremost, a *game of words*. And that should come as no surprise in an area where words lay strident claim to supremacy in an accent famous for its sing-song intonation.

Endless talking, one way of burning up the calories...

Pastis time: Taken at its most literal, this expression would mean "aperitif time". But this concept nevertheless has a meaning that is *cultural* inasmuch as the *pastaga* in question invariably conjures up images of a cool, shady arbour, and a reward after a game of *pétanque* played in the heat of the sun. In fact, there is a certain life-style that goes far beyond the narrow framework imposed by the first, simplistic translation. "Pastis time" is perhaps first and foremost an opportunity to call a large number of things into question - and certainly not "in the worst possible way"!

A way of life...

VINEYARDS AND COASTLINE

La Ciotat, Saint-Cyr-les-Lecques, La Cadière d'Azur, Evenos, Le Beausset, Le Castellet, Bandol, Sanary-sur-Mer, Ollioules, Six-Fours, Le Brusc

La Cadière (meaning "chair" in Provençal dialect),
a superb village set in the heart of a fertile wine-growing area.

VAR BEGINS...AT LA CIOTAT

Travellers who have read our previous work, **WONDERFUL PROVENCE**, will have noted that the coastline of the *département* of Bouches-du-Rhône was described in a west-east direction, stopping at Cassis! The decision to exclude the town which saw the birth of the *cinema* (invented, as we all know, by the Lumière Brothers) and *pétanque* may have come as something of a surprise. There is no doubt that the pretty little town of Cassis delights its visitors with its bijou marina, and with the string of tiny islands and creeks that form a veritable umbilical cord between it and Marseilles.

La Ciotat, on the other hand, is like the first movement of a symphony of sandy beaches which give the coastline of Var its special character, until you reach the "interlude"

at Toulon. Mind you, the town that stands on the site of the ancient city of **Cytharista** is not limited to the splash of emerald green waves forming a background to the blue shadows of the sunshades. For, near this seaside paradise, at the foot of a strange, and enormous rock justifiably called *The Eagle's Beak* lies a *real town* which, for many years, huddled not round the usual bell-tower but around the giant cranes that slashed the azure blue sky like the lead between the lights in a stained glass window.

Those were the days when nobody would have dared to weaken the economy of our beautiful Provence by preferring the shipbuilding yards of the Atlantic, or even the far-distant Baltic, to the ones along the shores of the Mediterranean. The harbour, though, is still there, beyond the town of La Ciotat whose narrow streets lined with small shops and boutiques open out onto the wharves se

Page 10: *Le Castellet, a mediaeval village near Bandol.*

La Ciotat, where the game of French bowls was invented, was famous for many years for the ships launched down its slipways.

between plane trees and the sea, once criss-crossed by rails and overlooked by the gigantic cranes with giant grabs that dug into the holds of monstrous ships. Nowadays, there is no noise to disturb those sitting on a shady terrace in front of a café and looking at the yard. The only sounds are an occasional, but intense, sound like a gong which is instantly muffled, or a hiss that is as brief as it is unexpected. Yet in its enormity, it resembles the thunder of an invisible forge worked by Vulcan in person.

In between these occasional rumbles and convulsive wheezes, there is not a sound! Nothing, except the ridiculous noise of the exhaust pipe of a motor bike on the quayside, or the whistle of a percolator in a café, a young girl's laughter, the clatter of high heels, the echo of a conversation carried on from one table to another, the chink of coins in a saucer, the rustle of a newspaper, in short, the thousand and one sounds that made up the thick, moving silence which once formed the background to my happiness.

This is silence such as is heard nowhere else. Silence that you can only hear on the quaysides of the harbour in La Ciotat where glorious but early autumns produced brilliant cradles of russet leaves for the boats about to go down the slipways...

A FAMOUS VINEYARD... BENEATH AN EQUALLY FAMOUS SUN!

The vineyards of Bandol produce an *Appellation d'Origine Contrôlée* wine which enjoys a fully-deserved reputation for excellence. It is, though, produced in an area

Steeply-sloping streets decked with flowers - this is another view of Le Castellet.

that actually includes seven other towns i.e. Saint-Cyr, La Cadière, Evenos, Le Beausset, Le Castellet, Ollioules and Sanary. Hence the statement once made by the boisterous master wine-grower of Saint-Cyr, Gaston Prébost,

Flower-growing in Ollioules (Var).

A view of the island of Les Embiez.

"You know, we (he was referring to the producers in the seven towns concerned) *produced the wine and, so as not to be left out, they gave it their name!"*

Saint-Cyr-les-Lecques, the most westerly town in Var, is both agricultural thanks to the fertile land around Saint-Cyr and a tourist centre with hotels along the superb Les Lecques Beach extending into pine woods dotted with campsites. And you can add to all this the delightful little yachting marina called *La Madrague*. A trip along the road to La Madrague is highly recommended; it gives an opportunity to see the archaeological wonders in the *Taurentum* Museum.

Another small town in the Bandol area is Evenos whose 10th-century castle stands high above the impressive *Ollioules Gorge*, at the end of which is the small town which gave the ravine its name. Ollioules has the largest flower market in France.

Returning quickly to Le Beausset, take the small road that wends its way through the vineyards and on down to Bandol via Le Castellet, a hilltop village that has attracted a number of far-sighted craftsmen. Le Castellet is a "must" on any visit. Opposite it is another superb village on the other side of the Marseilles-Toulon motorway, *La Cadière-d'Azur.*

Where Tango and Rumba reign supreme...

Bandol, a very popular seaside resort, has more to offer than just its yachting marina and its promenade full of boutiques, cafés and restaurants. It also has a casino happily housing, under one roof, the tiny roulette ball and its big brother, the ten-pin bowl. The casino already existed in the prosperous years just before the outbreak of the Second World War.

In those days, the streets of Bandol were filled with *Delages, Delahayes, Talbot-Lagos, Bentleys, Terraplanes Bugattis, Lincoln-Zephyrs* and other such horseless carriages, all coming and going from one dance hall to another, where their owners could dance the tango, the rumba, and the slow foxtrot. The best-known of these dance halls were *Poupoune, L'Amiral* or *Suzy.*

"Heavens! How beautiful they were, those inaccessible dancers stepping out of superb convertibles, accompanied by old men of thirty. We walked past them without really daring to look at them. We were ashamed of our shorts and our knees full of scrapes and scratches. Despite the rage that had us clenching our fists in our pockets, despite our carefree whistling, panic would have had us high-tailing it like rabbits if one of these "molls" as we called them revengefully, had even dared to smile at one of us."

Separated from Bandol by a narrow inlet of the sea, the island of **Bendor** boasts an interesting feature that is a cultural as it is popular with tourists i.e. the **Paul Ricard Foundation**. Bandol has given its name to the superb bay of which it forms the easternmost tip, yet most of the fine sandy beaches along the coast lie within the boundaries of Sanary... Note, on the "border" between the two resorts, a remarkable *tropical garden* containing a wide range of flora from every corner of the globe. The garden also has a number of animals and birds (parrots, apes, deer, llamas etc.), again brought here from distant climes.

THE TUMULTUOUS MARRIAGE OF ROCK AND SEA

Sanary is a peaceful resort reflected in the blue of the sea and sky. It has always been a resort for older people content with a gentle stroll and for children with buckets and spades. Its boats are sheltered within an enclosure where the sea is calm and its residents can enjoy an unhurried rest in one of its cafés with their pergolas and deep terraces.

Just as *Sanary* lays claims to "Bandol" Bay, so the small town of *Six-Fours*, its neighbour to the east, defends its rights to the seafront and the line of beaches which nevertheless seem to constitute, *the most naturally in the world*, an extension of the former Roman colony of Santa Nazarius which, in Provençal parlance, became better-known as San Nari. This "annexation" enables *Six-Fours-les-Plages* to claim on its tourist brochures that it has **11 miles of coastline, rocks, islands, rugged creeks and fine sandy beaches!** In addition to **three fishing harbours and marinas** and one thousand

The harbour in Sanary, a quiet corner of calm sea.

hectares of State forest! All this makes Six-Fours *the largest maritime community (and the most southerly) in France*.

Among the many tourist attractions in *Six-Fours* are the *Embiez Islands* (only a few propeller lengths from the "mainland") where the tireless Paul Ricard established not only an internationally famous yachting centre but also (in 1966) an *Oceanographic Foundation* which he set up with Alain Bombard; it specialises in environmental protection. High-quality hotel accommodation adds to the attractiveness of this heavenly little archipelago.

The main attraction, though, is *Le Brusc*, with the *Gaou* promontory, the final destination of this magnificent trip. *Le Brusc* began life as a simple seaside hamlet yet the surrounding countryside is more like a painting for artists with a deep love of colour than a series of post cards, often the only representation of places such as this. This is a maritime scene, where tranquil boats seem to be walking across a green sward of iridescent emeralds framed with white spume. On the other side of the path, on a bank shaded by pines with languorously overhanging branches, are the villas of yesteryear, each one a perfect background for a romantic story full of young ladies in crinolines and gentlemen in cravats and soft felt hats like those worn by artists.

Then comes the enchantment of *Le Gaou*, a rocky platform which, judging by the mouthwatering restaurant signs, is said to be the *Kingdom of Dame Bouillabaisse*. From the tip of the promontory (this is where the enchantment comes in), there is a view to port and starboard over a succession of creeks backed by breathtaking cliffs, themselves topped by luxurious tufts of green leaves. May you catch your first glimpse of this beauty spot on a day when, thanks to the mistral wind, the noise of the pebbles rolling in the undertow will blend with the long low moan of the waves breaking beneath the base of the rock flanked by white spume, in a marriage that has lasted since the dawn of time...

Olives, one of the main sources of income in Provence.

FROM SAINTE-BAUME TO THE SEA

Saint-Zacharie, Nans-les-Pins, Rougiers, Mazaugues, Le Plan-d'Aups, La Roquebrussanne, Signes, the Gapeau Valley, the Carthusian monastery of Montrieux, Méounes

The village of Méounes (Var) known,
in springtime, as the "Cherry Capital".

PILGRIMS' PROGRESS

Over the centuries, *Sainte-Baume* has suffered many an indignity and, because of this, it did not move an inch when, more than two hundred years ago, it was divided on the map with a dotted line that shared it out like a piece of cake between the *départements* of Var and Bouches-du-Rhône. The mountain range stretches from east to west over a distance of some 11 miles, rising to a height of 3,575 ft. at the summit. Because of the strange way in which it was divided up, the *département* of Bouches-du-Rhône has only two roads across it, one via Auriol and the other via Gémenos. The second of the two passes along the edge of the superb wooded parkland in Saint-Pons surrounding an old mill and its waterfall, and a very fine Cistercian abbey (unfortunately, not open to the public). Beyond it, in a series of hairpin bends winding their way through a landscape that has been eaten away by forest fires but whose very nudity gives it a grandeur all its own, the narrow D 2 road rises to the edge of the splendid cliff face forming the *Pic de Bertagne*, an incredibly white piece of limestone. The "tricorn hat" outline of this peak (alt. 3,380 ft.) stands out against a sky which, thanks to the seldom absent mistral wind, has a purity not seen anywhere else.

At the foot of the Sainte-Baume mountain range lies the Saint-Pons Valley.
St. Mary Magdalen's Cave on Sainte-Baume.

Lying on the mountainside at an altitude of 1,300 ft., *Nans-les-Pins* is a pleasant mountain holiday resort which fully deserves its name, since it is surrounded by pine forests that fill the air with the invigorating scent of resin.

The name *Sainte-Baume* brings to mind a number of pictures, including one of a superb forest covering an area of almost 140 hectares (this was sacred woodland to the Ancient Gauls) consisting mainly of giant beech trees but also including immense limes and impressive maples. Beneath the trees are the dark branches of holly, yew, spindle-trees, and ivy.

At the centre of the vast plateau to which it has given its name lies the village of *Le Plan d'Aups* and its Romanesque church. It is, though, the famous *St. Mary Magdalen's Cave* at the top of a steep path that attracts thousands of visitors every year, and they are not content with a brief stop at the *hostelry* run by monks. Every year, the pilgrims come to look at the cave ("*baoumo*", in Provençal) where, according to legend, the saint lived for thirty-three years. Another legend has it that *Master James*, the joint founder of the journeyman movement with *Soubise*, lived in the same cave but one thousand years later. The pilgrimage to the *Cave*, and the steep climb up *Saint-Pilon*, is a mandatory stage on the *Tour of France* that all journeymen must undertake as part of their initiation. It is during this trip that they *strike their colours*.

The mysterious lake known as Le Grand-Laoutien. Bauxite quarries in Mazauges.

The Sainte-Baume mountain range - rocks and boulders set against a background of greenery.

A LAKE FULL OF STRANGE CREATURES, AND A GREEN VALLEY

A short distance away from the final, eastern outcrops of Sainte-Baume is the mountain range called *La Loube*. Nestling at the foot of this 2,698 ft. mountain is *La Roquebrussanne*, fourteen letters to describe a peaceful village at the end of an immense plateau. It is surrounded by tenacious forests hemmed in halfway up the mountainside by a vast expanse of vineyard, forests which mark the boundary of a tiny verdant kingdom that enjoys an outstanding microclimate with exceptionally long hours of sunshine and a beneficial amount of rainfall. Together, they provide a type of irrigation that protects the forests from the ravages of fire.

Not far from the village, on the D 64 road in the *Garéoult* direction, is a signpost indicating the site of the *Grand Laoutien*, a sinkhole that is the only one of its kind in Europe. Some fifty years ago, in its inscrutable depths, a team of researchers found a dozen varieties of

The Gapeau and its fresh, fertile valley.

"gribbles", one of which can be considered as the cousin of the famous coelacanths, the wriggling prehistoric fish seen more recently in far-distant oceans, in fact a *monster* over three feet long!

La Roquebrussanne lies only a few miles from *Méounes* but we suggest that you take a quite different route to reach *Méounes*, namely the N 8 Aubagne-Toulon road then, beyond the *Camp du Castellet*, the D 2, a narrow road that unwinds gently through superb landscapes of woodland and thicket, the ideal place for picnics and football (or sweet nothings), until it reaches the village of *Signes*, of which Paul Ricard was Mayor for many years.

This wonderful tour will then take you to the narrow, cool, green *Gapeau Valley* where, shut in behind their walls, the monks of the Carthusian monastery in *Montrieux* sing praises to the Lord who was the Creator of this mini-paradise. Beyond the monastery is the small town of *Méounes*, long considered as the "Cherry Capital" and which, in springtime, offers visitors the magnificent sight one might expect, given its nickname.

Vineyards in the département of Var.

CANNONS, PALM TREES
AND ISLANDS

La Seyne-sur-Mer, Toulon, Le Mont Faron, Le Pradet, Carqueiranne, Hyères, La Capte, Giens Peninsula, La Tour Fondue, Porquerolles, Port-Cros, Le Levant

Port-Cros, "a nature reserve".

A typical Provençal market (Toulon)!

Wherever you are in the vast territory within the boundaries of *Six-Fours*, you will never be far from *La Seyne-sur-Mer*, the second largest town in Var as regards its population. *La Seyne* still bears the hallmarks of a rich industrial past (mainly due to its shipyards which are now shut). Its wharves face the ones along the seafront in the adjacent neighbouring city of *Toulon*.

MARINE CANNONS AND ARTISTS' PALETTES

Toulon, the largest naval base for France's warships, home port of the Mediterranean fleet and its aircraft carriers, was once infamous for its hard labour camps full of down-at-heel prisoners dressed in striped uniforms. Partially rebuilt after the last war, Toulon decided to draw down the curtain on a row of modern blocks of flats between its wharves and the lower end of its avenues, thereby creating a superb pedestrian walkway along the sea front. This part of the town is totally given over to maritime affairs, in particular the history of the French Navy (the *"Royale"*), through *Fort Saint-Louis, Fort de la Grosse Tour* (now the *Navy Museum*) and the *Armaments Depot* the linchpin of a military vocation that has lasted to the present day.

"The Tamarisks" near La Seyne-sur-Mer.

Toulon, though, also has an old town between the flow of cars driving along the Boulevard de Strasbourg and the quaysides we have just left. This is the main shopping area but it has more than just the myriad of shops and stores that first draw the eye. In the evening, customers return, but this time to the many bars and restaurants. The old town also includes a few streets that form the "*Chicago*" district frequented by sailors on shore leave who are attracted by the neon lights of certain signs.

It is impossible to talk about Toulon without mentioning its famous market along the Cours Lafayette, the prototype for the *Provençal markets* so beloved of songster Gilbert Bécaud. Toulon is also enjoying a prodigious intellectual and artistic boom, as is obvious from the *workshops* where, like the most famous of them all belonging to *Olive Tamari*, numerous painters, writers, philosophers, film directors, and actors could be found during the Occupation of France, all of them artistes who had fled the Nazis and their barbarity. Toulon, though, is also a *school of painting* represented in the past and still represented at the present time by artists such as **Baboulène, Sabatier, Morillon, Echevin, Salvado, Biancheri, or Segal** (to name but a few) and, of course, the master, *Olive Tamari*, an exceptional person who was both a painter and an outstandingly talented engraver and, at the same time, a wonderful poet.

"*I would never dare to dress in pale blue reminiscent of the greens of the happy days of the innocents nor become involved in the errors of young painters who see the sea as too blue in the blood red of the setting sun.*"

THE TIGERS OF MONT FARON

Toulon is almost impregnable from the sea, as it is from the landward side where it is protected by the impressive peaks that surround it. Among them are *Gros Cerveau, Coudon,* and *Mont Caume* but it is undoubtedly *Mont Faron* that has the most to attract tourists. There is a winding, but good, road up the mountainside but visitors can also use the cable car that whisks them to the top in just a few minutes. From there, they can enjoy a fairytale view of the city, its harbour dotted with the grey outlines of the fleet's aircraft carriers, the islands, peninsulas and green hillsides, all of them features of a very special landscape.

If you're hungry, *Mont Faron* has a range of establishments to suit every appetite. Including the appetite of the superb tigers born and bred in the lush enclosures of the *Mont-Faron Breeding and Reproduction Centre*. It is an impressive sight when these wild beasts, some of

them, such as the Siberian or Bengal tigers, absolutely gigantic, eat their way through a meal fit for... a tiger, of course! A large number of other big cats can be seen in separate enclosures, including leopards, black panthers, snow leopards, pumas, hyenas, and lynx, and there is an entire colony of chattering apes (the "*Bander-Logs*" so dear to Kipling's heart). Together, they make up a zoo which, although steeped in the scents of Provençal herbs rather than the smells of the savannahs, and resounding

"Chicago", one of Toulon's picturesque urban districts.

The marina in Toulon.

with the noise of crickets rather than the beat of the tom-toms, makes *Mont Faron* somewhat reminiscent of *Mount Kilimanjaro* — and a very pleasant reminder it is, too!

Don't leave *Mont Faron* without visiting the *Museum* set up in memory of the Allied landings in Provence in August 1944. Laid out in the old *Beaumont Tower*, the museum uses some spectacular audio-visual resources to give visitors an insight of what it was really like to participate in every stage of what was to be a turning point in the liberation of France, the Franco-Allied landing in Provence.

Before leaving Toulon, we must just mention its *Music Festival*, its *International Art Exhibition*, its famous "*Young Cinema Meet*" and all the other special events that are held in the ideal setting of the *Châteauvallon Cultural Centre* (set high above the harbour, it consists of an old castle, two open-air theatres, and an indoor auditorium with 600 seats).

Toulon, then, is home to the Navy. Toulon is the rustling, perky setting of the *Petites alliées* described so well by author Claude Farrère. Toulon is the home of the *red pompoms* and of artists dazzled by its colours. Toulon has superb houses, ideal for retired admirals, along the *Corniche du Mourillon* or on the *Cap Brun*. Toulon is full of winding streets (an "anti-mistral" device!) sloping gently down to the harbour. Toulon is full of colourful markets and fish or shellfish stalls redolent with the tang of salt and the scent of the sea air. Toulon-by-the-Sea is also Toulon-under-the-Mountains, a city that everybody always falls in love with — *so that those who know it are always torn between a desire to come back to it and a wish never to leave it in the first place*!

Toulon Harbour seen from the summit of Mount Faron.

OF FISHING NETS AND LINES

Beyond Toulon, the N 559 road lets its big sister, the N 98, provide a fast route to Hyères and the remainder of the Var coastline. This leaves it plenty of time to wander between the vineyards and the sea, creating an ideal route for those (like us, I suppose?) who enjoy "getting away from it all" in Provence. And what better place to do so than *Carqueiranne,* or *Le Pradet.*

Le Pradet is the first stop and, in the summer, thanks to its half-dozen campsites and four times as many hotels, its population quadruples. Residents and summer visitors alike can enjoy the superb seascape formed by a semi-circle of beaches and creeks separated by capricious lines of rocks, a paradise for anglers!

Beyond *Le Pradet* lies *Carqueiranne*! It is a pleasant resort with more than 4 miles of coastline and here again rocky headlands alternate with delightful little harbours. Doubtless considering that the title taken by *Carqueiranne* of **Sunniest Village in France** was insufficient, one of the redoubtable property developers creating a "Provençal Village" had no hesitation in informing possible purchasers, with the aid of gigantic signboards, that by buying a home here they would be able to enjoy *"the enchanting setting of the Pacific islands"*!

Far be it from me to criticise these fabulous strips of white sand and indigo-blue sea where the opulent fruit growing on the coconut palms is but a pale reflection of the busts of the lady holidaymakers. Personally, I am content with less; the sight of the anglers of *Carqueiranne* coming back early in the morning to the tiny harbour at *Les Salettes* is plenty for me. Even if the good old net lacks the exotic character of the native canoe, and even if it is the chink of bowls that can be heard beneath the plane

The "Corniche du Mourillon", a coast road dear to the hearts of the people of Toulon.

Carqueiranne, a small fishing harbour.

trees rather than the note of a ukulele. Even if the great priestess of this cult continues to be called *Fanny* like a character in a Pagnol novel, and even if the combined scents of garlic and aniseed are more popular here than the perfume of hibiscus. Even if the rooftops continue to display their pink tiles rather than green palms to the mistral wind. Even, and more especially, if *Carqueiranne* is only a few quarter-hours' drive away from home rather than a few hours' flying time...

LORDS, GRAND DUKES....
AND GOLDEN ISLANDS

Twelve miles of fine sand, thousands of palm trees, a profusion of flowers and tropical plants - this was how the pretty town of Hyères appeared in the 19th Century to the British aristocrats who first discovered it, quickly followed by Russian Grand Dukes. They could not have chosen better, for Hyères is the most southerly of all our coastal resorts. Hence the almost African vegetation, the superb gardens, and the climate that makes this a veritable paradise!

Hyères and its ultra-modern yachting marina.

Hyères, pride of the coast in Var.

In Hyères, though, all roads lead to the sea, its picturesque harbours and beaches, and its ultra-modern *yachting marina* (which has the added advantage of a nearby airport) extending into a natural geological curiosity, a double line of sandbanks forming an isthmus (*La Capte*) that links the *Giens Peninsula* to the Var coast. The peninsula was named after the village of Giens lying beneath the ruins of its castle on the top of a hill from which there is a magnificent panoramic view of the mountains around Toulon and the *Islands of Hyères*, otherwise known as the *Golden Islands*. The *Tour-Fondue* landing stage lies at the southeastern tip of the peninsula and is the embarkation point for people wishing to take the ferry to *Porquerolles* (less than twenty minutes away), *Port-Cros* (half-an-hour) and *Le Levant* (forty minutes).

Porquerolles, which is almost 5 miles long from east to west for a width that never exceeds one mile, is the largest of the *Islands of Hyères*. Its beaches and its tiny "harbour" (no more than a landing stage) lie along the curving northern coast, between the *Cap des Mèdes* in the east and the *Pointe du Grand Langoustier* in the west, as does the *village*, really no more than a vast square lined on three sides by the terraces of inns and running gently uphill to a rustic church.

The beaches at La Capte.

The "Main Beach" on Porquerolles.

Port-Cros, Fort l'Estissac built in the 17th Century.

There are very few motorised vehicles on the island. It is the haunt of walkers.... and cyclists. There are no roads running right round the island and even the humble footpaths that attempt to penetrate the thick scrub are quickly overgrown by a type of vegetation that defends the hilltops along the southern edge of the island with a pugnacity that is nothing short of amazing. The sight is breathtaking from every angle.

Port-Cros is smaller, and, on the map, it is shaped like a compact crab of unknown variety, the bottom of its back opening out to leave space for a tiny harbour while the north-western tip forms a huge pincer grasping the magnificent beauty spot known as the *Baie de Port-Man*. Like Porquerolles, *Port-Cros* looks out to sea along its south side, with impressive cliffs that are the haunt of seagulls and cormorants. But there is still some good walking to be done here, across the plateaux, beaches and valleys filled with exuberant flowers, where mastic-trees, arbutus and heathers form shady nooks that suddenly open up to show the rapid flight of a blue rock thrush or the swift dive of a peregrine falcon.

Port-Cros is a National Park, as is its tiny offshoot, the island of *Bagaud*. The park includes all the sea areas in this part of the archipelago, an area with an abundance of interesting species of animals and varieties of plants. This is a veritable biological treasure trove and it is covered by a protection order preventing the use of harpoon-guns or nets dragged along the seabed, and regulating the speed of boats.

The stretch of sea separating *Port-Cros* from *Le Levant* is scarcely half-a-mile wide; it is known as the *Passe de Grottes*. Le Levant consists mainly of a rocky backbone running from south-west to north-east over a distance of almost 5 miles. It is, though, only just over half-a-mile wide at its widest point, scarcely enough to carry the Navy's Guided Missile Test Centre which occupies the eastern half of the island. The south-west remains open to visitors and it is here that you will find *Héliopolis*, a nudist colony whose occupants are easy to distinguish from the naval and military men busying themselves with equipment that is often top secret - the nudists are the ones with nothing to hide!

On previous pages: *the cliffs along the Southen coast of Porquerolles.*

The Island of Le Levant, only 40 minutes from the mainland.

VAR, LAND OF VINEYARDS AND GREEN HILLSIDES

La Garde, La Valette, Les Trois Solliès, Besse-sur-Issole, Pignans, Notre-Dame-des-Anges, Gonfaron, Brignoles, Tourves, Le Luc, Le Thoronet Abbey, Carcès, Cotignac, Sillans-la-Cascade, Salernes, Entrecasteaux, Vidauban, Les Arcs, Le Muy, Draguignan

From the observation platform at Notre-Dame des Anges, there is a grandiose view of the Maures range.

When talking about their delightful little town, many older members of the community still declare themselves to be citizens of *La Garde de Toulon* rather than of *La Garde* in memory of the glorious past of a town long considered as "Toulon's lookout post". To prove it, it has a 12th-century feudal castle and a 12th-century fortified church, now a listed building.

As you travel down from *Mont Faron* eastwards to *La Valette-du-Var*, it comes as something of a surprise to find, so close to the city and in the heart of a densely-populated urban area, an old village nestling round its mediaeval church.

THE SOLLIES TRILOGY

Beyond *La Valette-du-Var*, the next stop on our trip is the green village of *La Farlède*, famous for the quality of its produce (flowers, fruit, olives and wine). Until 1878, La Farlède was called "*Solliès-Farlède*", thereby affirming its allegeance to the ancient *Soliers Estate*, i.e. to the illus-

trious *Forbin* family, one of the most powerful and influential in Provence.

Once *Solliès-Farlède* had broken away, there remained the solid trilogy of *Solliès-Pont*, *Solliès-Toucas* and *Solliès-Ville*. The first of the three developed from the 16th Century onwards, in the days when the *Forbins* came down from their eagle's nest in *Solliès-Ville* and settled in a castle built in the centre of a fertile plain.

Set apart from the main road, *Solliès-Toucas* is, in some ways, the "bridgehead" for the beautiful little road that crosses the *Morières Forest* (only a bell's throw away from the almost totally concealed Carthusian monastery of *Montrieux*) before joining the rural countryside on the *Signes Plateau* (which we have already described).

HALT, TRAVELLER, WEARY WITH HOPE...

The final part of the Solliès Trilogy is the small town of *Solliès-Ville*, although it does not consider that having "ville" (in French "town") attached to its name gives it pre-

A view of Solliès-Ville in the Var Plain.

Another view of the Maures mountain range.

cedence over its two sisters. Indeed, it looks kindly down on them from the top of the 970 ft. hill on which it stands. This is a veritable observation post, and it is proud of having been the adoptive home of *Jean Aicard*, poet and writer, author of the famous *Maurin des Maures*, a poacher with calves of steel and a heart of gold, as skilled at shaking off the gendarmes as he was at ensnaring game... and women!

Jean Aicard died in 1921 and bequeathed his house, aptly named "*L'Oustaou de Maurin des Maures*" (Maurin of the Maures' House), to Solliès-Ville of which he was Mayor. The town councillors turned it into the *Jean Aicard Museum* and a visit not only gives an interesting insight into the author's life but also provides a remarkable opportunity to see a real Provençal interior as it was in the days of *Frédéri Mistral*. Near the house is a church with a 15th-century organ considered to be the oldest in France. It also has a vividly-coloured 13th-century wooden Crucifix and two altar screens, one dating from the 15th Century and the other, a luxurious piece of woodwork and gold leaf, dating from the 17th Century. In front of the High Altar is a slab above the crypt where eighteen *Marquis of Forbin* lie buried. They were lords of this area and of many others in Provence. Among them is *Palamède,* the person who per-

suaded Charles III of Anjou to bequeath Provence to France.

While in *Solliès-Ville, the Town of Two Suns,* you can see a thousand other details ranging from a bust of the dramatic actor, *Eugène Sylvain,* to an effigy of the soldier-citizen, *Antonius Arena.* Be sure to continue along the road leading to the foot of *Le Coudon* (alt. 2,000 ft.) on the other side of the hill. From there, you will be able to see the entire plain around Hyères, the Saint-Mandrier Peninsula and the island of Porquerolles.

And there, if you are lucky enough to have beautiful sunshine and have had a small glass of rosé beforehand, you will easily be able to imagine yourself back in *Solliès-Ville* in front of l'*Oustaou de Maurin des Maures*, reciting these few lines by *Jean Aicard* that are engraved in the stone:

"Halt, traveller, weary with hope,
And, sitting on the threshold of this humble abode,
Fill your eyes and your heart with my vast horizon,
Nowhere else is Provence so fair!"

Almost systematically forgotten by guide books and tourist brochures, the good town of *Cuers,* a main town in one of the Cantons of Var, nevertheless has a population of more than 5,000, a figure which is perfectly laughable given the one that could be used to quantify the number of bottles produced every year by the local wine growers! This is the heart of the wine-growing area of Var, full of different names which are not in competition with each other but which intelligently complement each other (e.g. *Coteaux Varois, Côtes de Provence* etc.).

Situated, then, in the heart of a vast wine-growing area, Cuers also lies deep in the land that was once the haunt of *Gaspard de Besse*, the *"beloved brigand of Provence"* who robbed the rich to give to the poor. A journey along delightful little roads will take you to *Besse-sur-Issole*, the birthplace of the roguish *Gaspard Bouis*, who is said to have gained very early on in life a taste for "frolicking in the hay with the lasses and giving the gendarmes a right rollicking".

From Besse, you have a choice of joining the N 7 road by the direct route via *Flassans-sur-Issole* or of prolonging your tour via *Carnoules, Pignans* (the *"village of the thirty fountains and sixty flower-decked balconies"*).

There is a statue of a famous son of *Pignans* beside the boules pitch. His names was *Jules Gérard* and he gained fame as an army officier in Algeria just after the country had been conquered, where he was nicknamed *The Lion Killer*. Jealous tongues wagged and there were those who claimed that Jules Gérard killed more lions with his quill than with his rifle and that, if Daudet took him as his example when writing *Tartarin de Tarascon*, there was a reason for it. But the locals in *Pignans* answer, *"Yes, well, the people of Tarascon only have a copy, don't they? We have the original!"*

FROM LE CARAMY TO ARGENS

While in Pignans, it is well worth making a short detour through the forest to visit *Notre-Dame-des-Anges*. It is a particularly attractive outing, taking you up to an altitude of 2,600 ft. in an area containing the highest peaks in the Maures mountain range. *Notre-Dame-des-Anges* is a simple hermitage in memory of *St. Nymphe* (a young

A statue of Jules Gérard, the "Lion Killer", in Pignans.

The old town in Brignoles.

The Minifrance Theme Park in Brignoles.

Christian woman who was martyred in Rome) but it gives visitors an almost miraculous panoramic view from its terrace, not only over Sainte-Baume in the distance but, closer to home, the harbour at Toulon and, far away (in very clear weather, of course), Corsica.

From *Pignans*, our next stop is only 4 miles away, in *Gonfaron*, a sleepy little village that, over the past few years, has become an almost mandatory stop on any itinerary because of the setting up, in *Les Mayons*, of the now famous *Turtle Village*. The centre breeds turtles and tortoises in order to reconstitute the natural stock in the Maures range since *Chelonia* have often fallen victim to forest fires, urban expansion and collectors. Although it is illegal to collect the creatures, some five thousand of them disappear every year for this reason.

If you are coming from *Cuers*, which we have already described, you could, instead of passing through *Besse-sur-Issole*, have gone to Brignoles (via *Forcalqueiret*). This is a major agricultural and industrial centre and, when aluminium production was at its height, *Brignoles* was nicknamed "**the bauxite capital**". It has, though, retained another of its claims to fame, as the *capital of wines* because of its famous *Wine Fair*. Note, too, that

Brignoles is world famous for its marble. It was used as far back as Roman times (*Candelon*) and was chosen to face the base of the famous Statue of Liberty in New York.

The streets lined with prosperous shops have a well-satisfied air. On the squares, there are tables set out in the shade, giving passers-by an irresistible urge to stop and eat or have a drink outdoors. And this quiet little town has an undeniable charm. Added to this, there is the pleasure of strolling through its old streets, visiting its museum housed in the former Palace of the Counts of Provence or its wonderful *St. Saviour's Church* (*église Saint-Sauveur*) and, in passing, admiring the impressive *Templars' Gate* (*Porte des Templiers*) and the fountains whose incessant, centuries-old murmur symbolises to perfection the character of so many of the towns and villages in Provence which are facing up to the future all the more serenely because the past has provided them with such solid, tenacious roots.

Among the leisure amenities in *Brignoles*, one of the Var's sub-prefectures, is a famous go-kart track where future Alain Prosts have been battling it out over thirty years or more at the wheel of their small, but very fast, karts. There is also the very unusual "*Minifrance* theme park", a sort of scale model of the country including all its geographical and geological features and a total of 75 major sights, some of them (such as the famous *Carnac alignments*) natural, others due to the genius of man (*cathedrals, Centre Beaubourg* etc.).

Some seven miles west of Brignoles is the village of *Tourves* which undeniably attracts tourists thanks to the romantic ruins of Valbelle Castle. I suggest, though, that you take the street leading to the stadium then, leaving the stadium on your right, drive on until the tarmacadam is replaced by a simple dirt track running upstream along the banks of the *R. Caramy*. Walkers often have to stop on this narrow path to push aside an obstinate bramble, or bend down to avoid a branch lying across the path like a symbolic low doorway...

In autumn, the tumbling waters of the stream flow secretly into the depths of the greenery lit up by a veritable piece of stained glass foliage that filters the rays of russet sunlight dappling the *Caramy*. This highlights, in turn, the ballet played out almost on the surface of the water by trout diving and dancing between the stones...

Le Luc-en-Provence is a major junction within the *département* of Var, almost midway between Marseilles or Aix and Nice. There are other, similar villages, abandoned by a road (or motorway) which, after disturbing the peace for many years, now runs past some distance away. Yet there is nothing in common between *Le Luc* and these sleepy villages, beached hulls unoccupied other than by a skeleton crew! *Le Luc*, on the contrary, has an ever-increasing population and has remained a small town that has established a balance between a rich agricultural tradition (the area specialises in wine-growing) and a new economy witnessed in the successful creation of a number of flourishing industries.

Nearby is the well-known *motor racing circuit*, a very busy *Leisure Cantre* (tennis, crazy golf, sailing) and, of

The "romantic" ruins of Valbelle Castle in Tourves.

Le Luc-en-Provence is proud of its towers, with or withou a clock. Some are hexagonal, others square.

course, the countless *cellars* that make this region the holy of holies as regards *Côtes-de-Provence* wine. If, by any chance, you had the somewhat strange idea of watering down all this wine, you could do no better than visit the famous *Source de la Pioule*, a spring already known in Roman times. Not far from it are the remains of pump rooms with a 1900's casino serving as a reminder of the days when a langourous waltz would encourage gentlemen in panama hats to take in their arms languid creatures whose eloquently-swaying hips would belie the apparent innocence of a wide-eyed gaze and the austere rigour of an impregnable bun.

NEVER-CHANGING ARCHITECTURE

From Le Luc, cross over to the north side of the A 8 motorway and, a few miles further on, you will find yourself at another mandatory stop on any tour of this area - *Le Thoronet Abbey* which, with *Sénanque* and *Silvacane*, is one of the ***Three Cistercian Sisters*** of Provence. Situated a good league from the charming village of the same name, *Le Thoronet Abbey* complies fully with the Rule laid down by St. Bernard which demanded that communities build **"far from any town and always in a valley with an abundant water supply"**. In addition to strict observance of a Rule famous for its austerity, the monks complied with a never-changing architectural layout (Latin Cross with transept and two arms, semi-circular arches or slightly pointed barrel vaulting, supported by transverse arches) seen as a transitional stage between Romanesque and Gothic.

Here, as elsewhere, the appearance of Phrygian caps led the monks in their stiff white robes to flee, during the French Revolution, taking with them the echoes of the last Compline. Since then, every summer, the crickets have replaced them. Crickets, but also an association set up by the Ministry of Arts thanks to whom reminders of the genius of mankind such as this can be preserved and opened to visitors.

The austere splendour of Cistercian abbeys.

The superb village of Les Arcs-sur-Argens.
Cotignac and its cliff which is covered by a preservation order.

A pleasant 'A' road runs through the *Darboussière Forest* and on to the village of *Carcès* and the lake of the same name. Bordered over a distance of almost three miles by a lively little road that twists and turns in a delightful fashion, the 60-hectare lake is formed by the confluence of the rivers *Caramy* and *Argens*. That will give you some idea of the effect of the mere name of *Carcès* on the great family of men and women who plant their rods and lines on the banks, before fixing their flies, spoon-bait and appetising earth worms.

HOUSES SWALLOWED UP IN THE ROCK

Lost amidst the swelling tide of vineyards in Var is an incongruous name straight from Gascony - *Cotignac*. This is a village which, like the Paimpol of Brittany famous in song, is indissociable from the cliffs (they have been listed by the Fine Arts Department) of which the locals are, justifiably, more than a little proud. So proud, in fact, that they seem to have built the town in days gone by in such as way as to ensure that most of the streets have a glimpse of the cliff, forming a barrier dotted with caves and criss-crossed by flights of steps, a cliff 260 ft. high and 1,300 ft. long. Some of the houses in *Cotignac*, having tried just too hard to outdo their neighbours and build right up against the cliff face, have in fact been swallowed up in the rock, leaving only half the roof emerging from it, or a stretch of wall with windows in it, further along.

As to the houses that wisely kept their distance, their pebble dash and *Salernes* tiled roofs give them an air of wanting to perpetuate, through their bright, fresh colours, the appearance of solidity and healthy living that is *de rigueur* in an area where vineyards reign supreme.

Cotignac produces high-quality wines. Personally, I am particularly fond of the sparkling rosé-Muscat produced in the co-operative wine cellars here. There is not another one like it! As for good food, quality restaurants abound in *Cotignac*, the best of them all being a fine Provençal hostelry.

We shall speed up our journey slightly and arrive at *Sillans-la-Cascade*, a small village lapped by the waters

Fishing rods reign supreme in Lake Carcès.

of a tumbling river, the Bresque, that forms a waterfall here more than 130 ft. high. The *R. Bresque*, which rushes and tumbles along its course in *Sillans*, shows much less energy a few miles downstream in *Salernes*, a village to which, in the summer, it brings a pleasant coolness.

The wide avenues of Draguignan.

The "Saracen Tower" in Les Arcs.

Once a fortified town on the *Salt Route* (hence its name), *Salernes* still has a large number of ceramics factories specialising in the terra cotta tiles that are generally replacing the famous red *tommettes*, hexagonal tiles that provided the tiny village with all its wealth in days gone by and made its name famous throughout Europe.

Having left *Salernes*, but without leaving the course of the *R. Bresque*, we can now turn south along the D 31 road. Soon, the colossal *Entrecasteaux Castle* will come into view, "crushing" the village of the same name beneath its sheer mass, although the formal gardens designed by the landscape gardener with a magic wand, *Le Nôtre*, soften the austerity of this impressive aristocratic residence, once the seat of the famous family from which was descended Rear-Admiral *Bruni d'Entrecasteaux*, companion-at-arms of Suffren, who died off the Javanese coast while seeking the explorer, La Pérouse, and his crew who had been reported missing.

In the 1960's, the castle was purchased by a great Scottish painter, a Lord who, thanks to the work he undertook and completed, saved from absolute ruin the castle that had belonged not only to the *Entrecasteaux* but also to the Counts of *Grignan* and *Castellane*, all of them noblemen with whom, one may imagine, his own forebears (the Mac Garvie-Munn) exchanged a number of courtesies, with fist, musket or cannonfire.

Beyond *Entrecasteaux*, a very rural road leads to *Lorgues* (impressive 18th-century *collegiate church* with a painted marble High Altar, an organ built by *Zeiger*, and a *Madonna and Child* attributed to Puget) before continuing along a superb forest road (the D 48) to the town of *Vidauban* which gets its name from the Latin *vitis alba* ("white grape").

The next stop after *Vidauban* on the N 7 is *Le Muy*. This small town was once part of the County of Provence. In Roman times, animals were bred here for the circus in Fréjus. Since then, stock breeding has been replaced by other industries including the cork industry, once a major income-earner locally, although it never replaced the wine growing that is the main employer throughout this region.

If you drive a few miles back the way you have just come, you will arrive at *Les Arcs-sur-Argens*, a large village that is easy to spot since it is near the magnificent bridge carrying the N 7 across the R. Argens. The *Castrum Arcubus* of the days of Ancient Rome has an eventful history. In or around the year 1200 A.D, it was the birthplace of a young girl whose soul, thanks to Nature (or Providence, as you wish, and we know just how prodigal both have been in our fine Provence), was as splendid as her face and body were beautiful. The Church was to raise her to sainthood but, no doubt in order to keep up the sus

The hilltop village of Châteaudouble (north of Draguignan), standing high above the gorge of the same name.

On previous page: *Entrecasteaux'Castle has a garden laid out by Le Nôtre.*

pense, not until much, much later! Unaware that her virtues would one day bring her sainthood, the young lady of *Villeneuve* was even more deserving when she distributed to the poor of the parish the bread cooked up at the castle. And in order to escape the watchful eye of her miserly father, a miracle occurred each time he watched her leave the castle. As she walked away from it, the bread she held in her arms was changed into roses...

Nowadays, on the site once occupied by the castle, almost 3 miles from the village, stands an ex-abbey (*La Celle-Roubaud*), now private property. Only the abbey chapel (*St. Roseline's Chapel*) is open to the public. The beautiful giver of bread is buried here and we can see, perpetuated for all eternity, the illusion of an armful of loaves being turned into a bouquet of roses... In addition to modern stained glass by *Bazaine* and *Ubac* (representing rose petals, needless to say!), the chapel contains other works of art including an extraordinary tree-shaped lectern by *Giacometti*. The village produces a well-known wine in its co-operative cellars and has a few other surprises up its sleeve as well. Just a couple of miles up the hill is the "upper village" and the impressive *Saracen Lookout Tower*. Once you have seen all this, take time to stroll through the network of narrow streets lined with mansions each of them seemingly straight out of a dream full of National Lottery tickets...

Everybody knows that the mistral, the prevailing wind, excels in rushing across wide open spaces but is less keen on winding roads lined with high banks, thickets of fields planted with vines. All that makes its head spin until it loses its sense of direction and changes into a ridiculous breeze from nowhere, a wind good for nothing except to add a touch of freshness to the air. Hence the microclimate that makes towns like *Draguignan* so pleasant to live in.

Built at an altitude of 585 ft. at the foot of *Malmont, Draguignan* is surrounded by plants (palm trees, mimosa and cacti) that are quite the equal of what we have seen along the coast. It also boasts magnificent forests. Added to all this is the proximity of the incomparable Upper Var and its most outstanding scenic attraction, the *Verdon Gorge*.

FORESTS AND PASTURES IN UPPER VAR AND THE VERDON

Saint-Maximin, Barjols, Rians, Saint-Julien-le-Montagné, Aups, Villecroze, Tourtour, Ampus, Châteaudouble, Montferrat, Comps-sur-Artuby, the Verdon Gorge, Moustiers-Sainte-Marie, Sainte-Croix Lake, Aiguines, Bauduen

*The hilltop village of Châteaudouble
(north of Draguignan),
standing high above the gorge of the same name.*

Although the small town of *Saint-Maximin-la-Sainte-Baume* owes its name to the fact that it is considered (as we have seen in an earlier chapter) as the "gateway to the sacred mountain of Provence", its real origin dates back to the 13th Century when *Charles of Anjou, Count of Provence* began building the basilica and adjacent convent on the spot where a crypt had been uncovered containing the bodies, among other holy people, of *Maximin*, first bishop of Aix, and *Mary Magdalen* (who had come out of her cave for one last journey). With its "two-storey nave roofed with ogival vaulting" rising to a height of 97 ft. above the ground, *St. Maximin's Basilica* is the largest Gothic building in Provence.

SACRIFICIAL DRUMS AND FLUTES

Saint-Maximin is also the "gateway to Upper Var", opening onto the region via two roads, the D 3 to *Rians* in the north-west and the D 560 through *Seillons-Source-d'Argens* and *Brue-Auriac* to *Barjols* in the north-east. Known for many years as a major centre of the tanning industry, *Barjols* was also famous for the production of *drums and three-holed flutes*, both traditional instruments in the musical folklore of Provence.

A SORT OF MONT SAINT-MICHEL AMIDST THE SCRUBLAND

From *Barjols*, we head for *Tavernes*, a tiny village famous for the dryness of its climate. Indeed, it is so dry that never, in the memory of an asthmatic, has the slightest wisp of fog ever been seen there! Then turn left towards Varages (known in ancient times for its ceramics, which are still in production today) and on to *La Verdière* (a delightful village in the shadow of the huge castle that once belonged to the *Marquis de Forbin*). After that, another short hop takes us to *Saint-Julien-le-Montanié*.

Imagine a crumpled landscape of small valleys, covered as far as the eye can see with a green mantle of woodland and thicket. And suddenly, rising up from the centre of this sea of scrubland, you spy a sort of Mont Saint-

The basilica in Saint-Maximin.

A sort of „Mont Saint-Michel amidst the scrusland": Saint-Julien-le-Montanié: a proud village.
La Verdière, a village in the shadow of the Forbin family's impressive castle.

Michel in the form of a village not simply perched on a hilltop like so many others but rising up above the surrounding countryside as if lifted by an enormous wave... that has forgotten to come back to earth again.

Last century, this hilltop village lying at an altitude of 2,550 ft. had a population of 1,300 and a host of shops and cafés, and on market days its streets were crowded. Today, having lost nearly all its population, Saint-Julien lifts its head up to clouds steeped in memories while continuing to offer the unmoving splendour of silent streets and houses that are now "holiday homes" but which are still fine, upstanding constructions, proud of their cut stone and polished wooden doors, waxed smooth like a piece of furniture!

Downhill fom this aristocratic village and heading east, we pass *Montmeyan* and arrive in *Aups*, the main town in the Canton in this part of Upper Var, justifiably known as the *Capital of Truffles*.

The splendid village of *Villecroze* lies less than 6 miles to the south-west of *Aups*. It includes a listed beauty spot, and a series of caves, some of which are natural while others are manmade. To add to the attractiveness of the area, there is a cool waterfall and, downhill, a 2-hectare municipal park.

Tourtour and its superb fountain.

Opposite: *Villecroze, a waterfall in the very centre of the village.*

Châteaudouble Forest where Cigalou, the master charcoal-burner, could once be found at work...

Aups and its famous "carved rock".

Bargème, one of the most attractive villages in Var, and the one located at the highest altitude (1,097 metres-3,565 feet).

In Comps, the wheels at Auguste's watermill no longer turn...

A small road crosses the lush green countryside, showing an energy in line with the number of bends it includes as it climbs up to *Tourtour*, Villecroze' nearest neighbour known as the "Village in the Sky".

THE CHARCOAL BURNER AT FULL MOON

From *Tourtour*, the same brave little D 51 road led through *Ampus* famous for its car hill-climb to *Châteaudouble*, a village overshadowed by the impressive gorge to which it has given its name. But why the name *Château... Double*? The official version is based on what remains of a huge tower at the tip of the plateau and the scarcely visible line of battlements at the other end. There is, though, another, unofficial version. *Châteaudouble* is said to be a distorted form of *Castel Diaboli* , i.e. Devil's Castle!

Having given credit, for the benefit of the tourists, to the mistaken first version, the *Devil* can enjoy a quiet laugh at the bottom of a moat somewhere. So let's leave him to it and take a walk through this extraordinary village that once belonged to the Knights Templar. Their mark, or to be more precise, the mark of the journeymen-builders

The bridge over the Artuby in Verdon.

(the *Rosicrucian emblem, set square and compass*) is engraved into the pediment of many of the houses.

The time has come, though, to talk about the *Pranes Forest* not far from the village where, not so very long ago, my friend *Cigalou* still worked. He was the last master charcoal-burner in Upper Var. Now that he has gone, have the age-old techniques used to produce a uniquely pure charcoal been lost for ever? *Chi lo sa*? ("Who knows?") as the *carbonari* of old used to say.

Personally, I have been privileged to watch the building, in the magical *Les Pranes Forest* where the techniques used came from another age, then the lighting, *but only when the moon was full*, of one of the last charcoal kilns created by master charcoal-burner, François Cigalou, so that it burned for days and nights on end until, having completed its veritable *mutation*, it provided him with the *black gold* better known as charcoal...

FIELDS OF NARCISSI TURNED INTO FIRING RANGES

At the end of the Châteaudouble Gorge, beside the quiet village of *Montferrat* (the only sounds are the chink of *boules* and the song of the crickets), the D 555 crosses an area within the *Canjuers Army Camp* where you are not allowed to stop your vehicle until you reach *Comps-sur-Artuby*. In the 1970's, you could still take a stroll across the fields but since then they have been turned into a vast, *polygonal firing range* stretching from the banks of Lake Sainte-Croix in the west almost as far as *Mons* in the east, over a distance of almost 25 miles. *Comps, like its neighbour, Bargème,* is fortunate enough to lie on the northern edge of the firing range; *Brovès*, a delightful little village a few miles further south, was not so lucky. Expropriated and duly compensated by the Army, its population were forced to leave their homes, woodlands and pastures where sheep once grazed in their thousands. They also left to the rockets and mortar shells the fabulous fields of narcissi which made Brovès (its name has been deleted from any map less than 20 years old), in the right season, an island of happiness floating on an ocean of flowers.

A number of jokers (and there are jokers in *Comps* just as there are everywhere else) would have had me believe that *Canjuers* was not just a firing range but was also a hunting ground for military men and their guests and that the locals could hear grape shot being fired more often than mortar shells. They even went so far as to add,

"Our dogs, who luckily can't read, run between the sign-posts prohibiting access and head back wild boar and deer this way."

Having got all this off our chest, jot the name of *Comps-sur-Artuby* down somewhere as a possible venue for a visit or a longer break (alt. 2,925 ft, quality hotels and restaurants, Knights Templars' castle, campsite, fantastic *boules* pitch where 25 "*long*" games can be played at one time, not to mention forests, the river, mushrooms, honey, lavender, bread cooked over a wood fire etc.).

What was the bread like when it was made from the flour produced in *Auguste Chauvet's* mill? If we wanted an answer to this question, we would have to have come to *Comps* a few decades ago, in the days when the mill wheel was still turning, worked by the waters of the R. Artuby. Yet though it no longer operates, the wheel still turns - in Auguste's head of course, and in the mind of Josette, his wife. She, having heard all these stories so many times, has put them together in a book with the delightful title, *Tales from my Miller*. I suspect she may have taken this chance to prove that even when one is white-haired one can still

The Verdon Gorge and the famous observation platforms known as the "Balcons de la Mescla".

"Horsemen's Cliff".

be wonderfully in love with one's husband, *"a man with a gaze as blue as the waters of the river"*.

In order to replace the fruits of the earth with the fruits of the senses and the heart, Auguste and Josette now organise, at the mill 1 mile out of *Comps* on the La Bastide road, meetings between artists, poets and writers at the beginning of the summer. Oh yes, I forgot to say, Auguste and Josette have nothing to sell; they are rather more accustomed to giving. They are the sort of people who prefer to give than to receive. Survivors, one might say!

TALES OF JADE OR EMERALD

Comps-sur-Artuby is often suggested in guide books as the final stop on a tour in the area around the Verdon Gorge but here, on the contrary, it will be our point of departure. Before we set out, though, we should like to emphasise that this beauty spot *is unrivalled anywhere else*

From the very depths of the Verdon Gorge.

Moustiers-Sainte-Marie, capital of glazed earthenware.

Moustiers' fabulous Faience Museum.

Memories linger on of the monks who came from the abbey on Lérins to found Moustiers.

in Europe and that it is an entity in its own right. We shall not, therefore, take any notice of the administrative subdivisions which have put each of the shores in a different *département* (Alpes de Hautes-Provence on the right bank; Var on the left).

Take the D 955 from *Comps* to *Jabron*, stopping on the way at *Pont-de-Soleil*, from where we can see the full beauty of the Verdon Gorge with its tumbling, bounding waterway. This is also an ideal place from which to see the changes in colour (jade green in winter, emerald green in summer) performed by *this tumultuous tributary of the Durance*, which was born on the snow-capped heights of the *Allos Pass*.

If we had decided to leave *Comps* via the D 71, we would have reached the *Balcons de la Mescla* from which there is a view of the confluence of the rivers *Artuby* and *Verdon* (the view is particularly impressive from the 585-foot Artuby Bridge) then passed *Horsemen's Cliff (Falaise des Cavaliers)* and arrived at the *Corniche Sublime*, the high point of this indescribable wonder of the natural world, the Verdon Grand Canyon, a sight that invariably leaves you speechless. Whichever route you choose, you will have enjoyed a round trip that takes you to a place not to be missed — *Moustiers-Sainte-Marie*.

A KNIGHT AND HIS STAR

The name of *Moustiers* is synonymous with "fine glazed earthenware". Yet it was not until the late 18th Century that the industry gained a foothold in the small town that cuddles its houses between the sheer sides of two rocks strangely linked by a chain more than 650 ft. long decorated in the centre with a gilded star. The original chain died an understandable death through age and wear and was replaced in 1957 but it had been swinging over the abyss since the days of the Crusades. It was installed by one *Chevalier de Blacas*, a knight who had been forcibly turned into an immigrant worker in the land of the Barbary pirates and who had made this rather acrobatic vow to the Virgin Mary so that she would help him to regain his freedom.

Aiguines and its magnificent castle.

However, to return to the famous Moustiers faience, you must be sure not to miss a visit to the *Faience Museum* set out in an old, vaulted chapter house where you can see (but not touch!) priceless platters, plates, soup tureens, flowerpot holders, sweetmeat dishes and drinking fountains made by the great masters of the 17th and 18th Centuries, among them the *Clérissy family, Oléris,Laugier, Fouque,* and *Ferrat.*

When you leave this display of priceless pieces, you can console yourself for not having arrived two or three centuries earlier by making a few purchases from the current craftsmen in the locality, all of them as prestigious as their forebears. That is, after you have climbed the pilgrims' path to the amazing 12th-Century Romanesque chapel dedicated to *Notre-Dame-de-Beauvoir*, built over the remains of a 9th-century chapel said to have been constructed under the watchful eye of Emperor Charlemagne himself! The current chapel is well worth suffering cramp in the calves for, because of the panoramic view from the door and because

of the ornate decoration inside. Straight up above it, high in the blue Provençal sky, is Chevalier de Blacas' dazzlingly beautiful star, riveted onto its heavy chain stretched like an impossible wager above the abyss.

Lake *Sainte-Croix*, formed by a dam at the head of a "pocket" covering some 2,500 hectares, is divided lengthwise between the *départements* of Alpes-de-Haute-Provence and Var. It is on the bank within Alpes-de-Haute-Provence that you will find the village of Sainte-Croix from which the lake gets its name but it is on the Var side of the lake that you can see the village of *Salles-du-Verdon* which has been entirely rebuilt, since the original village disappeared beneath the water, as scheduled by the builders, when the dam was closed off. There are many beauty spots worth visiting in this area. Again on the Var side of the lake, there is *Aiguines* and its superb castle, and *Bauduen*, a village with houses backing onto the hillside yet so near the lake that their walls are reflected in its water.

Moustiers has a chapel built by Charlemagne!
The houses in Bauduen are reflected in the waters of the Sainte-Croix Lake.

THE MAURES RANGE AND THE SEA...
FROM HYERES TO SAINT-TROPEZ

Bormes-les-Mimosas, Le Lavandou, Cavalière, Le Rayol, Cavalaire, La Croix-Valmer, Ramatuelle, Cap Camarat, Gassin, Les Issambres, Saint-Aygulf, Sainte-Maxime, Saint-Tropez

*Brégançon Fort, an official residence of the Presidents of France
and a superb beauty spot on the coast of Var.*

REVENGE FOR CAMERONE.....
CUTTINGS OF MIMOSAS!

From February onwards, the greenery surrounding the stylish resort that has given itself the title of *The Most Flower-Decked Village in France* is decorated with dots of brilliant gold. So the best time to enjoy a visit to *Bornes-les-Mimosas* is at the end of the winter when spring is obviously just around the corner, although to tell the truth it is worth visiting at any time of the year! Especially as a tour of the village, set like a magnificent amphitheatre opening onto a superb panoramic view of the sea beneath the walls of the castle that belonged to the *Lords of Fos*, never takes very long. On the square is a statue dedicated to St. François-de-Paule who saved the townspeople from the plague in 1483. Chroniclers also suggest that it was not until the mid 19th Century, when the troops sent by Napoleon III to Mexico returned home, that the first tufts of mimosas flowered along the coast (this, however, is contested by some who maintain that mimosa comes from Australia).

More beaches, and another harbour, can be seen in the neighbouring town (built solely along the coast) of *Le Lavandou*. As far as the beaches are concerned, their names are *Saint-Clair, La Fossette, Aiguebelle, Cavalière* and *Pramousquier* and they provide over 6 miles of fine sand. As regards the harbour, it is from *Le Lavandou* that visitors make the shortest crossing to the islands. And, in addition to the famous *Corso Fleuri* in June, those who enjoy sea angling can take advantage of the tunny fishing trips which run almost right through the summer season.

From *Le Lavandou* to *Cavalaire*, the enchanting road known as the *Corniche des Maures* provides new delights at each twist, turn and bend. There is, for example, *Le Rayol* where there is a monument commemorating the Allied landings of 15th August 1944, and an extraordinary botanic garden lovingly tended by the *Coastal Conservancy Board* (*Conservatoire du Littoral*) and extending over several different properties. Their purchase, part-funded by Var County Council and the Regional Council, has saved this part of the coast, the *Corniche des Maures*, the most beautiful piece of coastline in Var, from the threat posed by property developers.

Back, though, to the *Corniche*, the coast road, and to *Cavalaire*, the westernmost tip of the bay of the same

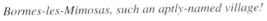

Bormes-les-Mimosas, such an aptly-named village!

name which is closed off on the other side by *Cap Lardier*, the southernmost tip of the *Saint-Tropez Peninsula*. At *La Croix-Valmer* (a listed village), turn off the D 559 that you have been following and right onto the narrow road leading to *Ramatuelle*, *Gassin* and *Saint-Tropez*.

If you want your name to go down in history, you are often obliged, whether you want it or not, to take a few short cuts that will create a public image which is always restricting. Such is the cemetery in *Ramatuelle* where, for an interval that is, alas! eternal, lies the body of the wonderful actor, Gérard Philippe. The village, though, is much more than a graveyard; it is built on the hillside and enjoys a prestigious panoramic view stretching from *Cap Camarat* in the south to *Cap Pinet* in the north and across the bay containing, with *Tahiti* and *Pampelonne*, the most famous beaches in the world.

The village of *Gassin* is listed. Its narrow streets unwind around the 715 ft. promontory on which it is built, decorated here and there with august arcades and monumental gateways. This layout may explain the constant tranquillity of the village, despite the never-ending flow of tourists. Yet *Saint-Tropez* is a mere 6 miles away.

The botanic gardens in Le Rayol.

In Le Lavandou, fishermen and yachtsmen tie up happily side by side.

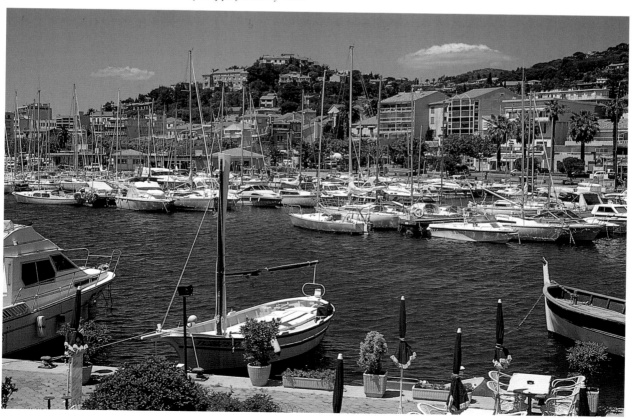

SAINT-TROPEZ, ONCE A LAND OF MILK AND HONEY!

Further east, i.e. on the "other side of the gulf" (a gulf to which the town, once the home of the illustrious *Bailli de Suffren* or "lou Baïle" as his crew called him, has given its name), further east, as we said, is *Sainte-Maxime*, a superb little town given fortifications and embellishments by the tireless *Monks of Lérins*. Facing the sea but, at the same time, with a network of paths and roads leading to a hinterland chosen by Jean Aicard as the setting for the exploits of **The Famous Poacher, Maurin des Maures**, Sainte-Maxime boasts a surprise *Museum of Phonographs and Mechanical Music*.

Back, though, to the town that we skipped over rather too quickly! A town whose name, as soon as it is spoken or written, brings with it memories of a string of famous beaches, slipping away like sand between the toes - *Pampelonne, Les Canabiers, Bora-Bora* etc. There are also a number of key words associated with it such as *Brigitte Bardot, Sénéquier, Vachon, Choses, le Gorille* etc.

This, as you will have guessed, is *Saint-Trop'*, a place much too well-known for me to insult you by giving you a guided tour! But there is also a large village which has somewhat fallen into oblivion, called *Saint-Tropez*, a place discovered just over a century ago by a few famous artists or writers such as *Signac, Dunoyer de Segonzac, Renan, Colette,* and *Maupassant* to name but a few.

In those days, the harbour was full of tartanes with multicoloured sails filling their holds with fine sand, wine, timber, cork, melons, water melons, silk cocoons and coral. In the hinterland, and on the deserted beaches, herds of half-wild horses could be seen galloping at will. One thousand five hundred head of cattle, and thirty thousand sheep grazed on the slopes of the *Maures*, the land of palm trees, orange trees, citron trees, giant aloes, Barbary fig trees, cork oaks etc. Here and there, you might see a steam-powered workshop turning briar roots into pipes, or cork into... corks. In the dense forests which were constantly cleared and, therefore, not subject to fire, there were eight hundred loggers and master charcoal-burners. Not to mention the shipyards (the harbour had a fleet of one hundred fishing smacks and every year one thousand ships would tie up here). There were flour mills, silver and lead mines, tile-making workshops and potteries, a flourishing liqueur and brandy industry, herds of white goats and wild boars, regiments of hares, foxes, and badgers, clouds of red partridge, woodcock, or quail.

So, before it became a "fools' paradise" as it is today, this really was a land of milk and honey..

Yet even if it is a fools' paradise, are there not some traps in which we willingly become ensnared? *Saint Trop'* is a perfect example.

Saint-Tropez and its harbour.

IN THE FOOTSTEPS OF MAURIN DES MAURES

Pierrefeu-du-Var, Collobrières, La Verne Carthusian monastery, Cogolin, Grimaud, La-Garde-Freinet, Bargemon, Fayence, Callian, Lake Saint-Cassien, Saint-Paul and Bagnols-en-Forêt, Fréjus, Saint-Raphaël, La Corniche d'Or

*The Maures and Estérel mountain
ranges share the azure blue of sea and sky.
Esterel Range seen from Cabris.*

*Pierrefeu: typical scenery in rural Var,
a land of villages and hills.*

*Holy Cross Chapel in Pierrefeu
Pierrefeu-du-Var, a famous vineyard.*

Pierrefeu-du-Var, which is easily reached from *Cuers*, a village that we have already mentioned, also lies in the heart of Var's vineyards and this entitles it to the *Appellation Contrôlée "Côtes de Provence"*. It also enjoys a reputation that makes its wine (in general terms, including all the wine-growing estates and co-operatives) one of the best there is.

Pierrefeu is also considered, and justifiably so, as a "gateway" to the *Maures mountains*. If you need convincing, just take the road to *Collobrières*, a pleasant road running through the forest along the banks of the *Réa Collobrier*.

Collobrier, like *Collobrières* , gets its name from a connection with grass snakes ("*couleuvre*" in French). Yet neither legend nor tradition has provided any story likely to establish a link, however tenuous, between the inoffensive serpent and this quiet little village famous for its glacé chestnuts. Unless the grass snake in question, overcome by its gluttony.... Well, you never know!

Continue along the D 14 to *Grimaud*, and just a couple of miles beyond *Collobrières* you will see a track forking off to the right (like the one in the fable, it is "*steep, rocky and difficult..*"). A signpost indicates that it leads to the Carthusian monastery of *La Verne*.

SERPENTINE, AN EXTRAORDINARY GREEN STONE

Perhaps, between the time these lines were written and the time you read them, the path will have been repaired. Even if it has not been, the destination is well worth ill-treating your shock absorbers for, spinning the steering wheel in all directions and "pedipulating" the foot pedals.

The spot "deep in the heart of the Maures mountains" often called "*African Provence*" because of its vegetation stretches over an area of almost 2 hectares. Far from any village, hamlet or mere farmhouse, this is the estate belonging to the fortress-like *Carthusian monastery* which still has traces of machicolated towers strengthening an outer wall designed, as in all Carthusian monasteries, to cut off from the world monks who have taken a vow of silence and meditation. Their cells, admirably well preserved and restored, are veritable hermitages. There is also the "*cubiculum*" (dorter), gallery, and workshop, all giving an insight into what life was really like for the volunteer recluses of days gone by. The panels grouped as if for an exhibition give visitors a large amount of information and take them round architectural gems inside and out ranging from an ornate Renaissance

The Carthusian monastery in La Verne, set against the dense forest carpeting the Maures mountains.

West Front to Romanesque doors on the chapel, and including the **serpentine** decoration in the small cloisters (serpentine is a stone with extraordinary green and bluish highlights in it), the dry stone arches in the main cloisters, the wrought iron work grilles, the carved woodwork, and the Gargantuan bread ovens in the main kitchens in the hostelry.

Returning to the winding but undoubtedly beautiful D 14 road, we arrive in *Cogolin, Grimaud* and, further on, in *La Garde-Freinet*. It is easy to remember that *Cogolin* is famous for its pipes and carpets; it is also well-known for its *reeds* (which are, to the clarinet, what the lips are to the mouth...). *Cogolin* has two famous honorary citizens, one the unbending *Clémenceau* (the General nicknamed "The Tiger" during the First World War) and *General de Lattre* (the *Liberator of August 1944*). By sheer coincidence, both men were born in Vendée, indeed in the same village — *Mouilleron-en-Pareds*!

Another view of a ruined feudal castle overlooking an attractive village with narrow streets can be had in *Grimaud*, which is full of *shop windows filled with treasure trove* and baskets of flowers, not to mention sudden glimpses of the green forests and blue sea in the distance. A fine public image, it's true, but people were obviously not satisfied with this *Grimaud* and, although it considered itself as the "*gateway to the mountains*", the *Grimaud* in question did not rest until it had used a part of the coastline over which it had ownership rights to build a town-marina (*Port Grimaud*) based on the vision of a *maritime architect*, François Spoerry, a man from Alsace who was haunted by the idea of moving yachtsmen nearer to their craft, finally designing the *most intimate* of dwellings that cater for both!

In *La Garde-Freinet*, you can take a stroll through cool streets and rest on café terraces on shady squares but the best walk of all takes you up to the rocky platform topped by the remains of a fortress dating from the days of the Saracen occupation (10th Century). This is an incomparable observation platform, rising to a height of 1,463 ft.

Fayence runs into *Tourettes* with which, for many centuries, it was engaged in conflicts that were nothing less than fratricide. It is a small town with much to offer, and it is well worth more than a quick stop, with a very wide range of activities. Among them gliding, a sport that has become so commonplace here that the sight of these great birds sailing silently across the sky is thought of as part of the scenery, just like the ring of the "*carreau*" punctuating the three steps forward taken by the players of Provençal-style bowls.

The gliders come from the Gliding Club on the shores of *Lake Saint-Cassien*, less than 6 miles away. A trip not to be missed!

The superb village of La Garde-Freinet set in the heart of the Maures range.

Fayence, a major gliding centre and a place to enjoy superb food.

A GIGANTIC FLAGON
BLOWN ESPECIALLY FOR THE QUEEN!

If you head due south from *Fayence* and drive some twenty miles, you will arrive at the ancient Roman town of *Fréjus*. First, though, you will have crossed the two small villages of *Saint-Paul-en-Forêt* and *Bagnols-en-Forêt*. This indication of woodland is fully justified for, in every direction as far as the eye can see, there is an infinity of hills and valleys covered with forests, mainly of oaks. And the locals say that this is nothing compared to what it used to be like! An elderly inhabitant of *Bagnols-en-Forêt* told me how, when he was young, he used to "go down" to Fréjus (a mere 15 miles away) "*walking under the trees without ever being in the sun*".

The story that I was told in the neighbouring village of *Saint-Paul* does not concern a walker but... a glass-blower. For many years, this village boasted a glassworks said to be so old that it would be reasonable to wonder whether the glassworks did not exist before glass was invented. One thing is sure - it existed during the 1350's when Good Queen Jeanne stopped in *Saint-Paul*. Yes, in *Saint-Paul*

where the master glassmaker was only too delighted to do the honours of his workshop by blowing for her majesty a bottle which he aimed to make more beautiful than any he had ever blown before. So he blew, but he blew so hard that, instead of a bottle, he produced an enormous, fantastic flagon worthy, of course, of the First Lady of Provence!

THE FINEST BEACH ON THE COAST

Our "forest" drive ends in *Fréjus*, a town much beloved of Caesar (**Forum Julii**) and an ancient maritime rival of *Massilia* (Marseilles). Thanks to its three miles of fine sand, *Fréjus* is fully justified in laying claim to the "finest beach on the coast". But this advantage may not have much value for it does not really go with the too frequent description of "garrison town" attached to Fréjus, a description that has been common from the days of the Roman legion to the times when Senegalese and Annamite infantrymen from French colonies were stationed here. Yet situated as it between the *Maures* and *Estérel ranges*, on a rocky plateau in the centre of a plain full of vines and fruit trees fertilised by alluvium deposits from the *R. Argens*, this town, with its population of 30,000, has a prestigious past evident in the ancient buildings that are the community's pride and joy. Traces of the Roman occupation include sections of town wall, its citadel-platform, its aqueduct, and its arena (the oldest in Gaul). *Fréjus*, though, was also a bishopric. This produced the 14th-century palace built of red sandstone from the Estérel range, its cathedral built over the remains of a 10th-century fortified church (probably, like St. Victor's Abbey in Marseilles, one of the oldest buildings still in existence in France), and its superb cloisters now housing an archaeological museum, part of which is given over to an outstanding collection of Gallo-Roman exhibits, the remainder being devoted to the fascinating history of *Old Fréjus*.

As the gateway to the *Estérel Range, Fréjus* also boasts a superb natural setting and, therefore, a seemingly endless list of places for walks and excursions. Among them is a trip taking in *Mont-Vinaigre, the Pic de l'Ours*, the State-owned forest, golf courses, and the fascinating *Estérel Safari Park* where you can drive through herds of wild beasts roaming free, with all your car doors and windows tightly shut.

There is, though, one memory that has not faded, the *dramatic breaking of the Malpassé Dam*. Today, although thirty years have passed since the catastrophe, people still crowd to the site, some of them mere sight-

Another perfect example of a hilltop village - Callian. The Maures range again, and its dense forest.

The terrible blaze at Le Tanneron. Martin Gray has not forgotten his family.

seers, others coming on a painful pilgrimage (access is via the Boson road). It was here, on the night of 2nd December 1959, *in a wave 162 ft. high*, that the dam across the *R. Reyran* broke. Carrying with it everything that stood in its way, the enormous wall of water (the reservoir stored fifty million cubic metres of water) took only 21 minutes to reach *Fréjus* a few miles further south. The death toll was frightening — 396 people were drowned or buried, and 50 of the bodies have never been found. A thousand buildings were totally or partially destroyed and 1,000 hectares of farmland were devastated.

THE GATEWAY TO THE DAZZLING "GOLDEN COAST ROAD"

The town of *Saint-Raphaël*, like its Siamese twin *Fréjus*, dates back to Roman times. Yet it was never a naval base, and it never had an armaments depot or a garrison. Nor, indeed, was it ever a bishopric. This explains why there are fewer ancient monuments here than in *Fréjus*. Unless you consider as a monument the pyramid erected near the harbour to commemorate

Fréjus and one of its major sightseeing attractions, the "Bishop's Town".

The cloisters alone are well worth a visit!

On previous pages: *The lagoon-town of Port-Grimaud.*

The Roman arena in Fréjus is the oldest one in Gaul.

The tragic Malpassé Dam.

Bonaparte's landing on his return from Egypt! Once he had become known as Napoleon and exchanged his General's bands for an imperial crown, the illustrious personage was, after a decidedly eventful career, to return to *Saint-Raphaël* fifteen years later, but this time it was to embark for the sad kingdom of the Island of Elba.

Valescure lies to the north of *Saint-Raphaël*. It has a golf course, superb villas and, nearby, the *Estérel Range* whose 20,000 hectares of forest offer an infinite variety of walks for car drivers smitten with a sudden desire to get out and stretch their legs.

Saint-Raphaël, though, is best-known as the start of the dazzling coast road that runs through towns with such prestigious names as *Boulouris, Agay, Anthéor, Le Trayas, Théoule* and *Napoule* , mile upon mile of splendid red porphyry until you reach the curving beach in the aristocratic town of Cannes.

Mount Vinaigre, the highest peak in the Estérel range.

Saint-Raphaël boasts a record 12 miles of beach!

Which are older, the bells or the Mediterranean-style roofs?
A creek along the "Golden Coast Road".

FROM LA CROISETTE
TO THE HAUTS-DE-CAGNE

Cannes and the Lérins Islands, Vallauris, Golfe-Juan, Juan-les-Pins, Cap d'Antibes, Antibes, Biot, Villeneuve-Loubet, Les Hauts-de-Cagnes

In Marineland, you might spot a "mermaid"
playing with the dolphins.

Considering the languid nonchalance with which the opulent town of Cannes unrolls its cut stone house fronts (aristocratic residences or mansions of another age that have been more or less converted), it is difficult to imagine that it was, over the centuries, besieged and pillaged on numerous occasions, by the *Moors*, the *Spaniards*, the *Austrians* and the *English*. Little remains today to remind us of this eventful history except the defensive bastions built on the *Suquet Hill* (its keep), the old Roman hillfort and the veritable "historic centre" of a town whose "history" does not merely date back to the building (fairly recently, since it is not even two centuries old) of the splendid seafront promenade known as *La Croisette* and the luxurious residential districts on the hillsides surrounding the town.

The history of the town of Cannes is closely linked to the activities of the *Monks of Lérins* and is, therefore, inseparable from the islands of the same name, of which there are two. The largest, and nearest, is *Sainte-Marguerite*, separated from the mainland by a strait only half-a-mile wide. The island runs from east to west over a distance of two miles and has a width of approximately 975 yds. On it stands the fortress in which the famous *Man in the Iron Mask* was said to have been imprisoned for years (open to the public).

Less extensive (1,625 yds long by 433 yds.wide), *Saint-Honorat* can be reached by boat, in a journey lasting half-an-hour (twice as long as for its sister island). Sights open to the public here include the *former monastery*, a veritable fortress with an impressive system of defence, built in the 11th Century by the monks to withstand recurrent raids by Saracen pirates. A number of chapels built for *hermits* are dotted across the island while at the eastern and

A star-studded venue in Cannes: the Festival Centre.

A luxury marina in Cannes.

western tips of land are two shot-ovens built on Bonaparte's orders in 1794. They serve as a reminder of a warring tradition that has, fortunately, become obsolete and which even the explosions of the fireworks set off to inaugurate or accompany the dazzling festivals and special events organised in the nearby luxurious town throughout the year do not seek to copy.

ROUND PLATES AND SQUARE FORTRESS...

It would be far from the truth to say that *Vallauris*, a small town that has become known throughout the world for its craftsmen-potters, is famous solely because it was here, in 1947, that the illustrious *Pablo Picasso* chose to live. And although the presence of the great artist helped to spread the fame of *Vallauris* over the decades, the reasons for which the highly-creative artist chose this particular colourful, bustling town are undoubtedly not based on sheer chance. It was in *Vallauris* that Picasso set up his *Temple of Peace*, inaugurated in 1959 in the old castle chapel. This vast allegorical work consists of two huge panels measuring 32 ft. by 15 ft. The *Picasso Collection* is on per-

Cannes is inseparable from the Lérins Islands offshore.

In Vallauris, glazed earthenware reigns supreme, in every shape and size.

The former monastery on the Island of Saint-Honorat.

Golfe-Juan and its beaches.

On previous pages: *La Croisette, the promenade of dreams...*

The superb frescoes in the Sanctuary Chapel in La Garoupe.

manent display on the first floor; it consists of two hundred and twenty works.

As we travel back down the hill from *Vallauris*, we come into view of the *Antibes* Peninsula which forms the boundary, beyond the *Pointe de la Croisette*, of a magnificent, sheltered gulf. The road crosses *Golfe-Juan* (don't blink or you'll miss it) then reaches *Juan-les-Pins*, an elegant, rustling resort in winter and summer alike, by day

and by night — indeed day and night run feverishly into each other here.

The eastern end of the gulf is marked by *Cap d'Antibes* which adds an appropriate note of tranquillity since this is one of the places selected by the world's royals and multimillionaires as a holiday venue. It is, then, amidst a silence broken only by the song of the crickets that, for one brief moment on a summer holiday, you pass fabulous mansions and inaccessible residences. Then, having passed the most famous of all the beaches, *La Garoupe*, we arrive at *Antibes* , "Antipolis" ("the town opposite") as it was called by the Greek merchants of Massalia (Marseilles) who founded it as an ideal centre from which to trade with the Ligurian tribes, because it was nearer than *Nikéa* (Nice). Nowadays, the *Antibes* region is dotted with a mosaic of greenhouses (more than three million square metres), making it one of Europe's largest flower-producing areas.

A visit to the old town of *Antibes* is a "must", including, of course, the cathedral (Romanesque chevet, 17th-century nave), and the impressive *Château*

The powerful lighthouse in Cap d'Antibes.

The Picasso Museum in Grimaldi Castle in Antibes.

The Square Fort in Antibes.

Grimaldi housing the *Picasso Museum*. Remember, too, that only half-a-mile to the north of *Antibes* is the world-famous *Fort-Carré* (Square Fortress), the final remains (with the *Front-de-Mer*) of the fortifications designed by Vauban.

In *Antibes*, though, music has pride of place, for example in the very well-known *Jazz Festival* held here every year. And we should not leave the town without a mention for the extraordinary *Marineland* amusement park situated on the *Biot* road at the junction of the D 4 and N 7. Its basins are home to a range of marine mammals and the highlight of the visit is an acrobatics display by impeccably trained dolphins.

Our next stop, after a very short drive, is *Biot*, which takes us momentarily away from the coast. *Biot* is a typically Provençal village, awaiting visitors on the top of a rise. As amusing as the dolphins that we have just seen, is a climb up and down its streets, past housefronts gleaming in the sunlight. It is famous for its pottery, a craft for which it has a well-established reputation, and *glassmaking*, a craft calling upon magnificently-preserved traditions and

the age-old skills of the glass blower to produce, at the end of his rod as inspiration takes him, wine glasses (the inimitable *Biot* "hand-blown glasses"), bottles, carafes, lamps, jugs etc.

It should also be remembered that *Biot* is becoming increasingly famous for its jewellery (some superb pieces are created here), that a famous golf club provides amenities second to none and that, last but certainly not least,

Antibes, the "beach-town"!

Biot is the home of the *National Fernand Léger Museum* housing almost three hundred and fifty works by this artist. He played an important part in the development of Cubism, along the same lines as Cézanne, then moved towards a form of representation which, if not totally figurative was at least a more concrete expression of everyday life, in the extraordinarily austere style that he made his own.

Another short detour inland will take us to *Villeneuve-Loubet*, where there is a very unexpected museum (although it is always a welcome sight) i.e. the *Museum of Culinary Arts*. Now a foundation, it is housed in the birthplace of the famous chef *Auguste Escoffier*, whose fame was so wide-ranging that he has gone down in history as a great ambassador of French cuisine (and, consequently, of France itself). The museum contains one of the most extensive collections of documents seen anywhere in the world.

The Fernand Léger Museum in Biot.

Orcs in Marineland, Antibes. © Jacques Foudraz.

The famous glassworks in Biot.

The lavish Castle Museum in Les Hauts-de-Cagnes (modern art).

Villeneuve-Loubet and the Escoffier Museum of Culinary Arts.

WHAT IS LEFT
OF THE "MONTMARTRE OF THE RIVIERA"?

Thanks to a patient, centuries-old policy of buying land, the powerful, noble *House of Grimaldi* became accustomed to monopolising the Land Registry, one might say, over a vast region extending from the *Marquisate of Les Baux* to what we now know as the *Principality of Monaco*. So it is hardly surprising that it is, yet again, the name of *Grimaldi* which is linked to the foundation of the superb castle in *Les Hauts-de-Cagnes* at a time when "*residential land development*" was almost unknown. Nowadays, the old castle has been turned into a *Museum of Modern Mediterranean Art*, making *Les Hauts-de-Cagnes* not only a centre of art and culture but also one of the region's main settings for special events.

Housed in the wonderfully ornate rooms of the luxurious castle belonging to the *Grimaldis*, the museum was set up just after the Second World War and has the

most unusual of all collections (including the *Suzy Solidor Donation*). There are forty portraits of the famous, eccentric singer by artists ranging from *Foujita* and *Van Dongen*, to *Lempicka, Kisling* and *Dufy,* not forgetting *Cocteau, Brayer, Domergue, Marie Laurencin, Picabia, Christian Bérard* etc. The museum,

The museum in Les Hauts-de-Cagnes.
Forty portraits of actress Suzy Solidor.

Les Collettes, the house (now a museum)
that once belonged to the artist, Renoir.

Les Collettes - a view of the house.

though, cannot be mentioned without a word about its great curator, now deceased, *Jean Clergue*, responsible, among other things, for the setting up of the *International Art Festival* held every year in Les Hauts-de-Cagnes and thereby giving a perennial flavour to the nickname of "*the Montmartre of the Riviera*" once given to this hilltop village.

In those days, the narrow streets in the old village resounded with the familiar clank of the old, rickety cart on which *Soutine* used to transport the badly-framed canvasses that he exchanged for a bowl of soup!

In addition to its marvellous castle-museum, the village of *Les Hauts-de-Cagnes* has the famous *Maison des Collettes*, the house in which *Auguste Renoir* worked and died, now the most fascinating of museums, in which, *since everything has been left in its place*, there seems to be no reason why the old man should not suddenly rise from limbo, wrapped up warmly, and seating himself back down in front of his easel, pick up between his arthritic fingers a brush on which the paint has refused to dry.

Those were the days when the view stretched over the deep green of the olive trees or the sparkling nudity of the fine sandy beach rather than over absurd pyramids of concrete...

WHERE ROADS
AND PERFUMES MEET

Mougins, Sophia-Antipolis, Valbonne, Roquefort-les-Pins, Saint-Paul-de-Vence, Vence, Tourettes-sur-Loup, Les Gorges du Loup, Le Saut-du-Loup, Gréolières, Gourdon, Grasse, Saint-Vallier-de-Thiey, Les Gorges de la Siagne, Saint-Césaire-sur-Siagne

Gourdon, a village that seems to be balancing on the top of a 2,600-foot cliff.
The gardens round its mediaeval castle were laid out by Le Nôtre.

Saint-Paul-de-Vence (photo by Hervé Boulé).

The Car Museum and its ultra-modern layout (Mougins).

The best road from *Cannes* where we were earlier is the N 85, the **Napoleon Road** taken by the emperor when he landed in *Golfe-Juan* after his stay on the Island of Elba which he obviously did not enjoy. Less hurried than His Imperial Majesty (he, after all, had a throne to win back), today's visitors can take time for a few detours which, from *Mougins* (now a place famous for its good food where guide book stars and chef's hats are legion), will take them to the famous *Sophia-Antipolis Science and Technology Park* (the *crème de la crème* of high tech) or, nearer *Grasse*, the hilltop village of *Opio*, which lies beyond *Valbonne* (be sure to see the beautiful arcading round its main square).

Grasse is a major road junction. It can also be reached by the D 2085 (via *Villeneuve-Loubet* and *Roquefort-les-Pins*) but it is at *Cagnes-sur-Mer* that we shall start, on a tour that takes in *Saint-Paul-de-Vence*, *Vence*, *Tourettes-sur-Loup* and *Gourdon* (via the splendid *Gorges-du-Loup*) before returning to *Grasse*, a magnificent drive if ever there was.

TOURETTES-SUR-LOUP SHARES WITH TOULOUSE THE TITLE OF "VIOLET CAPITAL OF THE WORLD"

These days, the addition of "de Vence" to the name of Saint-Paul does not imply any vassaldom. And without going so far as to speak of "competition" between the tou-

rist attractions in each of the villages, let us simply say that *Saint-Paul-de-Vence* and *Vence* have a diversity that allows them to complement each other.

To take but one example, it is an interesting fact that, thanks to the extraordinary *Maeght Foundation*, the old village of *Saint-Paul* with its town walls still intact gives

The Rosary Chapel in Vence.

Sophia-Antipolis, a look into the technological future and the 21st Century.

Saint-Paul-de-Vence and its prestigious Maeght Foundation.

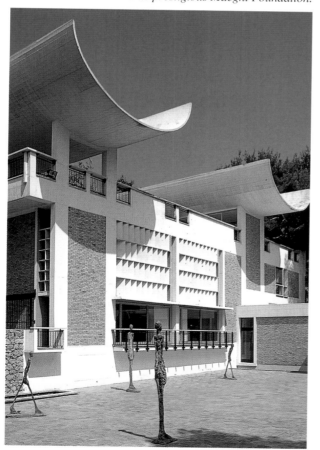

On the Place du Frêne in Vence, the gigantic tree dates back to the 16th Century!

visitors an incomparable view of *Modern Art* while set on a hillside in the neighbouring town of *Vence* is a piece of work entirely designed and built by *Henri Matisse*, the outstanding *Rosary Chapel."*

Built on a spur of rock at an altitude of 1,300 ft, *Tourettes-sur-Loup* is only a few miles from *Vence*, which no doubt explains why the famous "residential land development" has spread so vigorously here that a mere rabbit hutch costs as much as a house with a good plot of land round about it elsewhere, and not necessarily all that far away! It should be said, though, that although I mentioned "rabbit hutches", the term cannot be applied to the very fine *St. John's Chapel* in which the frescoes painted by *Ralph Soupault* are a real masterpiece of Naive Art. They recount the Old and New Testament through characters that are, in fact, portraits of villagers! As to the artist, he is so modest that he has signed his work only with a humble violet, a flower which brings us quite naturally to the plant that has brought this luminous village its wealth from centuries back, and still provides a few families with a living today. Yes, *Tourettes-sur-Loup* shares with Toulouse the title of *Violet Capital of the World* and it is from here that a veritable harvest of fresh bouquets is sent out every year, to sweetmakers and florists' shops. The flowers are picked from October onwards, until in March they enter the period of full bloom, making this one of the most spectacular floral sights anywhere.

A game of pétanque in Saint-Paul-de-Vence (photo by Hervé Boulé).

Tourettes-sur-Loup challenges Toulouse for the title of "Violet Capital of the World".

At the *Pont-du-Loup* beyond *Tourettes*, we shall turn "upstream" into the *Gorges-du-Loup*, generally considered to be one of the most interesting natural curiosities in Provence. The tumbling stream rises in the outcrops of the Alps near Grasse and, justifying its name ("loup" means "wolf" in French), seems to have had to carve out a passage for itself by biting great chunks out of the mountainsides surrounding it.

Just after the *Gourmes Waterfall* stretched like a curtain against the sheer cliff of a wall of limestone, there is the first tunnel. Beyond it, you can see the first "water spectacular" — the *Demoiselles Waterfall*. Unless you prefer to continue to the typically Provençal hilltop village of *Gréolières* lying down the mountainside from the resort of *Gréolières-les-Neiges* that is so well-known to skiers, you can, once you have passed *Le-Saut-du-Loup*, cross over to the other bank of the river and head back towards *Gourdon*, a mandatory stop on any tour.

Although it has become very banal, the term "eagle's nest" really is the most appropriate description of this extraordinary beauty spot. Imagine, balanced precariously on the very top of a cliff 2,600 ft. high, a village with a determinedly mediaeval appearance, its austerity softened by gardens that look as if they, too, are suspended in mid-air, designed by none other than the great landscape gardener, *Le Nôtre*.

And *Grasse* is only some six miles from this fabulous "hilltop village".

ONE OF THE MOST BEAUTIFUL FLOWER MARKETS IN THE WORLD

Any visit to *Grasse* must start at the *Place des Aires* in the old town. This picturesque square in the shade of the nettle-trees is decorated with a fine fountain of three

The Gourmes Waterfall in the Loup Gorge.

Gourdon, or when "one flew over an eagle's nest".

The three basins on the fountain on the Place des Aires in Grasse.

Fragonard's "patriotic" frescos in the stair well of the Fragonard Museum.

stone basins and surrounded by houses over arcades. It is here that, every morning, a flower market is held — arguably one of the most beautiful flower markets in the world! From the square, you can go along narrow streets and vaulted passageways (many of them filled with shops and shoppers) and up flights of steps to the cathedral. Among other priceless items, the cathedral contains three paintings by Rubens and, above the door to the sacristy, one of the few "religious" paintings by *Fragonard*, tending to prove that this talented local lad did not find in churches the inspiration that he drew from the dimness of a bedchamber. The stairwell in the museum is also admirable. It is decorated with patriotic motifs with a symbolism similar to that of the obelisk erected over the *Four Lions' Fountain* in the centre of the Place du 24-Août near the cathedral. There then remains the traditional visit to one of the perfume factories that make *Grasse* the perfume capital of the world. Meanwhile, and afterwards, its wide avenues will have given you a

glimpse of the slopes of the Estérel Range, and the creeks and beaches along the coast.

And, as one cannot live solely from paintings and perfume, you will be sure to find one of the restaurants offering specialities based on the abundant local produce such as *artichokes à la Barigoule*, incredible *asparagus or courgette batter puddings*, or a recipe for stuffed cabbage leaves known here as *Sou façoun*. All this can be followed by a substantial *steak and shallots* and washed down by either a *Coteau de la Gaude* or a *Côtes de Bellet...*

THE GLASS USED BY THE EMPEROR

When he landed from the *Island of Elba*, via *Golfe-Juan*, Napoleon chose to cross the Alps , *"in order to hop from church tower to belfry until he reached Notre-Dame"*, ignoring the Rhône Valley because, although there were no

The perfume industry brings Grasse its fame and its wealth.

bell-towers in that area, there were on the other hand rather too many hostile troops. This being so, once the Emperor had passed *Grasse*, he found nothing but rough mule tracks. Luckily, times have changed and great quantities of tarmacadam have covered the pathways of History. The *"Napoleon"* Road is now worthy of the person after whom it is named.

Like your illustrious predecessor, you can stop in *Saint-Vallier-de-Thiey*, a village set amidst meadows and woods where the greenery forms a stark contrast to the rugged, rocky slopes round about rising to heights of 4,875 ft. The village enjoys a calm yet invigorating microclimate and has much to offer in the way of excursions, sightseeing (ruins, swallow holes, dolmens, hillforts, barrows, Romanesque chapels, wild ravines, tumbling rivers and dense forests). This makes *Saint-Vallier-de-Thiey* a pleasant resort which, rather than being listed among the "popular tourist venues" that fill this region, is merely (and this is what gives it its special charm) an ideal *summer*

holiday resort, especially for those in search of a *real holiday*!

But holidays must have been far from the mind of the hurried traveller who, one day in March 1815, stop-

Even (or perhaps especially) in Grasse, drunkenness does not come from just any bottle...

ped here for just a few minutes with his suite, at a local inn. He accepted the glass of wine offered to him by the innkeeper, but only after the latter had taken a mouthful himself, to prove that the drink was not likely to deprive the *Bonaparte* family of the most noteworthy of its sons.

As they listened to the story later on, rich travellers sometimes asked whether the glass from which the Emperor had drunk (it was displayed in a glass cabinet) was not for sale. Then, in order to overcome the final scruples of the innkeeper, the inveterate collectors would take out their purses full of coins.

It is said that the wily innkeeper sold hundreds of copies of the glass from which the Emperor had drunk, thereby making himself a fortune, but he was still less wealthy than another local named Réal. This time, there was no question of a glass; it was a mule. When the Emperor left Saint-Vallier, he and his followers started to climb the steep path up the *Siagne Gorge*, at nightfall. On a path such as this, the first slip is inevitably the last. Heavily laden with a trunk containing gold and silver

coins, one of the mules did just that and disappeared into the dark abyss.

Time was at a premium and the mule and trunk had to be considered as lost by his Peripatetic Majesty. The peasant named *Réal*, though, left Napoleon to head for *Saint Helena via Waterloo* and managed to recover the contents of the trunks. Having done so, he became the richest and most important land-owner in the region.

IN THE MEANDERS OF A CAVE

It is at the foot of the *Audibergue*, a mountain lying in one of the bends of the Napoleon Road between *Saint-Vallier-de-Thiey* and *Escragnoles* that you can see the spot where the *R. Siagne* rises, at an altitude of more than 3,250 ft. It then runs down to the Mediterranean, flowing into the sea near the famous resort of *La Napoule*. Before ending its course like the rich, however,

The famous "Roman Wells" in Saint-Cézaire.

Overleaf: *The Saint-Cézaire Caves in the meanders of a world set in stone.*

the bright little mountain stream enjoys every possible twist and turn, even running along the boundary between the *départements* of Alpes-Maritimes and Var for part of the way. It marks the border when it runs through the gorge to which it has given its name, below the pretty village of *Saint-Cézaire* which, from the spur of rock some 1,072 ft. high on which it is perched, seems to be gazing in awe at the wild, tumbling waters. And the stream maintains the same swift pace as it crosses woods, plateaux and forests.

Saint-Cézaire-sur-Siagne has a fortified gateway called the *Roman Gate* that opens onto the low streets. There is also a 14th-century fortified gateway known as the *Tower Gate*, a Romanesque chapel that is a listed building and that contains a superb sarcophagus and a mill that produces very high-quality oil. Meanwhile, the former flour mill has become a "Mill Museum" containing permanent exhibitions of pain-

tings, sculptures, stained glass and Provençal costumes.

At the other end of the village from the gorge are the famous *Roman wells of Saint-Cézaire* which, because of their stone roofs, are reminiscent of the stone shepherd's huts called *bories*. In all, there are nine of them, some roofed, others open. The largest has a diameter of more than 23 ft. and the water reaches a depth of almost 20 ft.

The last part of your visit demands a degree of bravery — the famous *Saint-Cézaire Caves*! A guide will take you down to caves 162 ft. below the surface, in a strange, labyrinthine world of concretions. The skilful use of lights, coming on in just the right place at just the right time, will show you the full extent of the fantasy world that Nature is capable of producing. There are not only the conventional stalactites and stalagmites but, thanks to the red clay, lime and iron magnesia, a range of shapes and forms that is a staggering sight.

NICE TO MENTON
THE SPLENDOURS OF THE RIVIERA

Nice, Villefranche, Saint-Jean-Cap-Ferrat, Beaulieu, Eze, La Turbie, Cap d'Ail, the Principality of Monaco, Beausoleil, Roquebrune-Cap-Martin, Menton, Gorbio, Castellar, Sainte-Agnès

Nice: a town with a population of more than 400,000 overlooking "Angels' Bay".

Since it is fashionable at the present time for shops to indicate their opening times as "7 days a week", the city of Nice could justifiably lay claim to a highly significant "365 days a year". Although tradition handed down over the years tells us that, at the turn of the century, the English aristocrats and Russian Grand Dukes, some fleeing the icy banks of the *Neva* or *Moskova* and others seeking to escape the London fog or the thick *Highland* mists, waited until winter came before spending their *roubles* and *pounds* here, it is quite different these days when, thanks to seminars and conferences, one "Season" swiftly follows another.

It is true that, in winter and summer alike, this city of 400,000 people can enjoy the enchantment of a superb panoramic view with the *Baie des Anges* as its setting and the mountains steeped in ermine white and azure blue forming the backcloth.

In Nice, a dried up river bed, the *Paillon*, contains the foundations of major, and magnificent, buildings such as the *Exhibition Centre*. The other particular feature of the *Paillon* is that it cuts the city in half, with the modern city to the west including the famous *Promenade des Anglais* reached by motorway and the *Nice-Côte-d'Azur Airport* (the second busiest airport in France as regards its number of passengers) and leaving the old town and harbour in the eastern half of the city.

Following a line that runs approximately from north to south like the *Paillon*, the Avenue Jean Médecin (once called *Avenue de la Victoire* in the heady days that followed the Great War of 1914-1918) has an impressive row of shop windows. It leads to the superb *Place Masséna* on which the arcaded houses with yellow ochre façades give this major location in Nice some of the haughty charms of *Florence* although we are never allowed to forget that the "ex-County of Nice", now the "Nice Area", owes nothing to *Tuscany*, or to any other region on the other side of the Alps however fine they may be. And so it has been since a plebiscite held in 1860!

Apart from the Place Masséna named after the glorious general nicknamed by Napoleon, "*the favourite child of Victory*", Nice has another superb square, this time named after another of the town's glorious sons, Garibaldi! As if to celebrate the exploits of this tireless freedom fighter, the square is decorated with a statue of the famous leader of

Nice: the Promenade des Anglais backs a long line of beaches.

the *Red Shirts*, surrounded by a splendid decor of fountains and flower beds.

With the *Quai des Etats-Unis* beyond the *Promenade des Anglais*, it is (symbolically at least) the dollar that reinforces the attractions and benefits once paid for by pounds sterling, a currency that has lost some of its financial clout in the modern world.

Lying parallel to the Quai des Etats-Unis is the famous *Cours Saleya*, one of the "gateways" to the old town. It is famous because it is used for a dazzling flower market, an early vegetable market offering produce that is not found anywhere else, and a fascinating bric-a-brac market. It also has a series of inviting terraces (cafés and restaurants).

It is impossible to talk about the old town without mentioning the many restaurants that fill its streets and, more especially, what you are likely to find in your plate.

What makes cooking so different in Nice is the subtle balance between two traditions — seafood and produce from the mountains. Moreover, and in both cases, local

The market on the Cours Saleya, a veritable institution in Nice.

Place Masséna and its huge fountain.

High above the old harbour in Nice is "Castle Hill", where reminders of ancient history abound.

people use only the very best of produce, ingredients whose incomparable quality comes from Nature at its most generous. Here, you will find really fresh fish, octopus and other such small calamaries, with a profusion of vegetables of all kinds, and a flavoursome olive oil, all of which is accompanied by a wide range of herbs. Not to mention the back-up of fresh pasta prepared in a thousand and one ways with as many sauces, pasta that can stand its own in the face of competition from its Italian cousins. Pasta is served for the *"méranda"* (the snack eaten in the morning when the fishing fleet comes in) but can be replaced by the well-known *"pan bagna"*. There is also the *"pissaladiera"*(an anchovy, olive and onion quiche), or the mouthwatering *socca* (pancakes made with chickpea flour).

At table, you can enjoy a *bagna cauda* (raw vegetables dipped into a fondue of hot olive oil, garlic and anchovies), a *trouchia* (herb and Swiss chard leaf omelette), the famous *ratatouille*, fresh *gnocchis* or ravioli, tripe, beef stew *"à la niçoise"* and *porchetta* (stuffed sucking pig). Not forgetting the *poutine* and *nonats* (elvers served fried or in a salad), and the pinnacle of local cuisine, the surpri-

sing (perhaps because of the smell?) *estocafida* or *Stockfisch*, a stew made of ungutted smoked haddock cooked with garlic, onions, new potatoes, tomatoes, peppers, and the miniature olives found nowhere else but Nice known as *pichiolinces*!

Having completed our gastronomic interlude, we shall return to the harbour which we have already mentioned. This is a major part of the link between the mainland and Corsica, hence the seemingly endless line of cars that wait, when the evening ferry is in, to be "swallowed up" by the monstrous car decks as they are nearly every day. Because this is a sight to be seen almost in the town centre, it is a favourite destination for people out for a stroll, and a sight much enjoyed by the diners sitting in the restaurants around the harbour.

To the west, the harbour extends as far as the *Colline du Château*, once the site of a fortress (it was demolished in 1706), and now the setting for cool waterfalls that are skilfully and attractively floodlit after nightfall.

Back, though, to the seafront, i.e. the *Promenade des Anglais* ("*lou Camin del Inglès*") which, although we are talking about nothing more than memories, continues to

Nice harbour seen from "Castle Hill".

conjure up, in the impressive hotels and luxury residences that line it, a past that has succeeded in adapting to a present which is by no means poverty-stricken!

Luckily, in Nice (where the supreme weapon is a caustic humour almost akin to derision), everything ends in frenzied entertainment. There is the traditional *Carnival* which begins on a Saturday ten days before Pancake Tuesday. During the two weekends of this carnival period, there are parades of floats and people wearing disguises and masks, battles of flowers or confetti, fireworks displays and dances (where the wearing of a mask makes it possible to take a few good-natured liberties) before the effigy of His Grotesque Majesty is finally burnt on a bonfire.

In Nice, more than anywhere else, the exact meaning of words is of paramount importance. When it comes to "festivals", the corresponding number of "seasons" obviously exceeds four! In fact, it would a thankless task to try and draw up an exhaustive list of the festivities and entertainments that are staged here throughout the year. And just as difficult to draw up a full list of all the buildings, churches, chapels, museums, theatres, galleries,

exhibitions, festivals, sporting events etc. There are so many of them that choice is vital, but take care to choose wisely! We shall, then, leave it to guide books and specialist brochures to list them all.

On the north side of the harbour, bordered by the hillsides of the *Paillon Valley* and the hills, dotted with luxury villas, of *Mont-Alban* and *Mont-Boron* are the working class suburbs of *Riquier* and *Saint-Roch.*

On the other side of the double line of avenues, jetties and boulevards bordering the enclosed course of the *R. Paillon* and forming very useful means of avoiding the worst of the traffic is the residential district of *Carabacel* extending northwards into the aristocratic district of *Cimiez*. From the hilltops dotted with luxury houses, the *Chagall Museum*, the no less fascinating *Matisse Museum, Roman arena, Roman baths,* and the ex-*Celementum* of the Romans (they had a garrison here that was totally independent of *Nikaïa*, a harbour considered to be under the influence of the merchants of Massilia, or Marseilles) all seem to be ostentatiously indicating that this is a sort of "town within a town" set well away from the noise, hustle and bustle, a town that has its own, eventful story to tell.

Nice - the Matisse Museum.

The *Paillon Valley* and the hilltops of *Cimiez* lead to the superb hinterland which we shall discuss in detail later.

THE SPLENDOURS OF THE RIVIERA

Less than 25 miles separate Nice from the Italian border, and to reach it you have a choice of three different routes — the Lower, Middle or Upper Coast Road (*Corniche Inférieure, Moyenne Corniche* and *Grande Corniche*). In order to follow the coast as closely as possible and visit all the seaside resorts, we shall take the first of the three and our first stop will be the very fine town of *Villefranche*.

This is an old town which, thanks to its citadel, its network of narrow streets, its steep flights of steps, its vaulted passageways and its dark corridors round about, has retained a decidedly 17th-century atmosphere. Its small fishing harbour and marina open onto a bay justifiably described as the "most beautiful bay on the Mediterranean coast". The water is never shallower than 81 ft; in some places it

Nice - the Roman arena in Cimiez.

Nice - the Chagall Museum.

The name of Villefranche is linked to that of a bay considered to be one of the most beautiful in the world!
The old town and citadel in Villefranche.

Beaulieu and its strange "Bay of Ants".

On previous pages: *The Ephrussi de Rothschild Villa and its lavish gardens in Le Cap-Ferrat.*

even exceeds 195 ft. This, then, is an area that can shelter entire squadrons and the dozens of warships.

The western end of this immense bay is formed by the *Cap-Ferrat Peninsula*. A circular road lined with luxury mansions leads to the tiny village of *Saint-Jean-Cap-Ferrat* (originally a mere fishing hamlet) and, from there, rejoins the coast road. A few miles further on is the elegant resort of *Beaulieu*. First, though, we must stop and visit the *Fondation Ephrussi de Rothschild*, otherwise known as the *"Ile de France" Museum*, a reference to the famous liner on which the donatrix, Madame Maurice Ephrussi, née Béatrice de Rothschild, enjoyed numerous cruises, while spending most of her time collecting the fabulous works of art now displayed thanks to her heir (the French Academy of Fine Arts) in the magnificent residence built for her in the middle of a fairytale group of "gardens on a theme" (*tropical, Japanese, Mexican, Florentine* etc.).

Almost "inextricably linked" to *Saint-Jean-Cap-Ferrat* and its peninsula, and sharing its well-heeled clientele, *Beaulieu* is both a summer and winter resort which, thanks to the hills that protect it from the cold northerly winds, enjoys an exceptionally mild micro-climate that is greatly

appreciated by its residents when the winter winds are blowing. Note, too, the perfect reconstruction of a rich Ancient Greek mansion, the *Villa Kérilos*, which was bequeathed to the *Institut de France* by the famous archaeologist, *Théodore Reinach*.

Beyond *Villefranche, Cap-Ferrat* and *Beaulieu*, the road runs along the foot of the magnificent hilltop village of *Eze* some 1,365 ft. above. The village can only be reached from the middle coast road, and this is quite understandable. Eze is a perfect eagle's nest, and its has a very interesting *Tropical Garden* (300,000 visitors every year) topped by the remains of a 14th-century castle.

Eze-Village is complemented by the seaside resort of *Eze-Bord-de-Mer* which lies amidst pine and olive trees on the lower coast road where we were to begin with. For the moment, let us continue our "high-altitude" excursion and head for another mediaeval village, *La Turbie. Mont-Agel*, which has a famous golf course, is not far away. It rises to an altitude of 3,737 ft.

La Turbie owes much of its popularity with tourists to its famous "*Trophée d'Auguste*" (or "*Trophée des Alpes*") erected by the Romans after the death of Julius Caesar to commemorate their conquests throughout the alpine region. From the monument, there is a vast panoramic view of the *Principality of Monaco* and the rocky coastline down to the Italian headland of *Bordighera*.

Back on the lower coast road, we cross *Cap d'Ail*, a name that refers to both the promontory concealing Monaco from view and a pleasant town situated in the heart of an unspoilt natural environment of cliffs, creeks, and coastal footpath. Note that *Cap d'Ail* has an open-air theatre decorated with mosaics by Jean Cocteau.

A WORLD WHERE "EVERYTHING THAT THE SALT OR OZONE COLOURS"...

A palace (lived in by princes and princesses) with guards who seem to have stepped straight out of the pages of a children's book, an *Oceanography Museum* that is undoubtedly one of the finest in the world, *Tropical Gardens* that attract 50,000 visitors every year, a harbour filled with sparkling white yachts, millionaires who seem to have been created specially for life in the luxury mansions next door to the *casinos* that create ex-millionaires,

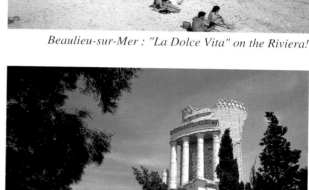
Beaulieu-sur-Mer : "La Dolce Vita" on the Riviera!

The Alpine Trophy in La Turbie.

Eze, a hilltop village that is the pride of the Riviera.

tower blocks rising to ever more dizzy heights and the astronomical price of the land on which they are built, a *world-famous rally* and a string of fast cars noisily jockeying for pole position in the most popular of all the *Grands Prix*, a *tournament* that attracts the very top, and wealthiest, experts in passing shots and straight backhands, a football team with no financial worries, and citizens (sorry, "subjects") who do not know what income tax is, an *Opera* with a number of beautifully-formed ladies consti-

tuting a renowned *corps de ballet...* these pictures all come to mind as soon as somebody says the magic words, *Monaco* or *Monte-Carlo*.

We must, briefly, stop for an explanation that will probably complicate rather than simplify matters. *Monaco* is the name of a *principality* of which *Monte-Carlo* is only part, as is *Le Rocher*, otherwise known as *Monaco-Ville*, where the prince lives in his (obviously princely) palace. Then there is *La Condamine*, the harbour district extending beyond *Sainte-Dévote*, *Fontvieille* built on land reclaimed from the sea as a result of a recent (and gigantic) civil engineering project, and *Moneghetti*, the hilltop residential district including the entrance to the *Tropical Gardens* and the *Parc Princesse Antoinette*.

All that remains, as we have seen, is *Monte-Carlo*! It is the easternmost part (including the beaches at *Larvotto*) of this tiny sovereign state. Monte-Carlo contains the most famous hotels (or, to be more precise, those that have been the best-known for the longest time) and the legendary *Monte-Carlo Casino*. In the area between the *Casino* in the centre and the two venerable institutions to each side, i.e. the *Café de Paris* and the *Hôtel de Paris*, is a long

Monaco's Oceanography Museum.

The tropical gardens in Eze.

Cap-d'Ail's open-air theatre was decorated by Jean Cocteau.

stretch of lawn rising gently to *Beausoleil*, a locality situated "on the other side of the border", in France! The long green sward is called the *Boulingrin*, a deformation of the English "bowling green". Nowadays, though, people are content to enjoy *roulette, craps, baccara, black jack* and the inevitable slot machines. Among the many attractions offered to visitors and residents by the principality, there are the lush *Tropical Gardens* where you can see, among other plants, several thousand varieties of cactus, and an *Oceanography Museum* that enjoys a worldwide reputation for excellence. It was set up at the turn of the century by *Prince Albert I* , himself one of the greatest oceanographers of his day. This is a place not to be missed, with a zoological oceanography room filled with the impressive remains of great marine animals, and an aquarium where, with mouths gaping behind their glass walls, fish from every corner of the globe, gaze at these strange bipeds (with no gills) who come to see them and reassure themselves, no doubt, that the world in which they live really is eternal, as described by the poet José-Maria de Heredia in his lines:

The Prince's Palace in Monaco.

A view of the "Rock" (the town of Monaco).

The harbour in Monaco.

The much-prized residential area of Roquebrune-Cap-Martin.

Opposite, top: *Monaco's famous casino.*

Opposite, left: *A statue of the "Navigator-King", Albert I of Monaco.*

Opposite, right: *The cathedral containing the tombs of the royal family.*

"...Where everything that the salt or ozone colours,
Moss, tangled algae, anenomes, or sea urchins,
Covers in dark purple and sumptuous designs
The vermiculated bed of the pale madrepore..."

A TOWN "WHERE EVERYTHING IS GOVERNED BY THE SUN"

"It's a delightful little town with a somewhat unreal atmosphere, where everything is governed by the sun..."

It was in these terms that the English novelist, Katherine Mansfield, described *Menton*. And the author of *The Garden Party* and *The Doll's House* is also said to have used another expression whose simplicity is a perfect definition of this exquisite town, *"My town is a garden!"*

In this town, in which, as people like to point out, there is an infinite number of *"exceptional* gardens", you can see thousands of varieties of flowers and plants creating enchanting forms and colours round villas built in terraces up the hillside. And it is obvious that the talents of the gardener are akin to the genius of an inspired painter.

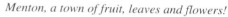

Menton, a town of fruit, leaves and flowers!

There are also palm trees growing with a vigour unlike anything seen elsewhere on this side of the Mediterranean coast, thanks to the incredibly mild microclimate, not to mention the pines, olive trees and cypress. Then, one might almost say, "not forgetting" the citrus fruit groves which ensure that, at the right time of year, the constantly-green backdrop to Menton is dotted with thousands of golden or russet fruits, all of them celebrated at *mardi gras*

The hilltop village of Le Castellar.

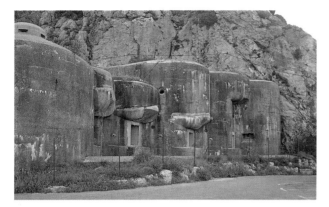

with the traditional, but nevertheless unusual, *Lemon Festival.*

The Alps, which remain at a reasonable distance from the coast for many miles, cannot contain themselves any longer and here, at the final outpost of the French coast, they seem to want to rush headlong into the sea, whether or not they are topped with the hilltop villages that give the hinterland its specific character. Among them are the extraordinary old villages of *Gorbio, Le Castellar,* and *Sainte-Agnès* , a "*coastal village* (it lies only two miles from the sea) *that is the highest in Europe* (altitude 2,457 ft). The village has a population of 945, occupying an area of 937 hectares! Faced with the threat of invasion from the east, the area was given the southernmost sections of the *Maginot Line* (it was more fortunate here than its big sister along the eastern border!). *Fort Sainte-Agnès* is part of this system, designed for a long, patient period of waiting, like the mythical "*Fort Bastiani*" described by the great Italian writer *Dino Buzatti* in his immortal work *The Tartar Steppe.* There, too, the fortress was designed to keep watch over identical, almost deserted stretches of desert.

The old fortifications in Sainte-Agnès.

The old fortifications in Sainte-Agnès.

ERMINE WHITE AND AZURE BLUE
THE HINTERLAND OF NICE AND MENTON

Peille, Contes, Coaraze, Col Saint-Roch, Notre-Dame-de-Bon-Coeur, Luceram, Peïra-Cava, Turini, L'Escarène, Levens, Tinée Valley, Saint-Sauveur, Valberg, Auron, Isola, Valdeblore, Saint-Dalmas, Saint-Martin-de-Vésubie, La Madone-de-Fenestre, Le Mercantour, La Madone d'Utelle, Le "Saut des Français", Sospel, Briel, Saorge Gorge, Saint-Delmas-de-Tende, La Vallée des Merveilles, Notre-Dame-des-Fontaines, La Brigue, Tende, The Little Train of Les Pignes

A hinterland studded with villages: Peillon.

Peille, a "mediaeval curiosity".

The church in Contes contains the admirable St. Mary Magdalen Reredos.

In a previous chapter, we covered the *Grasse area* including the *Gorges du Loup* and the *Siagne Gorge*, even climbing up to the ski slopes of *Gréolières*. Then, following the plan laid down for the previous book, we visited the beautiful city of Nice and continued our trip along the coast to Menton and the nearby hilltop villages.

We now have to visit the hinterland of the Riviera, being careful not to distinguish between the "hinterland of Nice" and the "hinterland of Menton"! We have preferred, instead, to use the *natural* divisions within this admirable countryside created by the various valleys which, beneath the same azure sky as the *Riviera* dig out a passage for themselves between the mountaintops dressed, in the winter, in an ermine white cloak. The main valleys are *La Tinée, La Vésubie,* and *La Roya.* Then, although travelling further to the *Mercantour National Park,* we shall be sure not to miss the less northerly beauty spots and villages which are more easily accessible from the coast.

In fact, we shall begin with them.

Luceram, an old fortified village.

Coaraze: a sundial by Cocteau.

A LAND WHERE THE VILLAGES PLAY TIG

Situated some six miles west of *Sainte-Agnès* where we made our last stop, the village of *Peille* is a veritable *mediaeval curiosity*, an impression that is further heightened by the narrow, cobbled streets interspersed with flights of smooth worn steps and by the vaulted passageways. It would come as no surprise to turn a corner and find oneself face to face with a halberdier.

In the hinterland bordered by the Var Valley to the west and the Italian border to the east, there is a large number of old hilltop villages, all of them obviously interesting. Some have a chapel or church, others have a square embellished by an old fountain, others again a vaulted porch or a pavement whose stones seem to be resounding still to the clank, forgotten elsewhere, of the iron-clad wheels on the carts of days gone by.

Such a village is *Contes*, built on a spur of rock 11 miles from the sea. To get there, take the D 2204 road north of Nice via *Drap* then turn onto the D 15.

Beyond *Contes*, the tiny D 15 (otherwise known as the "Sun Road") takes us to *Coaraze*. We have travelled only

Turini Forest, an incredible labyrinth of trees.

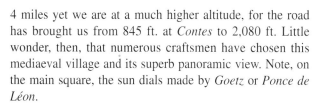

L'Escarène and its old bridge over the Paillon.

Opposite: *The Mescla Gorge in the Tinée Valley.*

4 miles yet we are at a much higher altitude, for the road has brought us from 845 ft. at *Contes* to 2,080 ft. Little wonder, then, that numerous craftsmen have chosen this mediaeval village and its superb panoramic view. Note, on the main square, the sun dials made by *Goetz* or *Ponce de Léon*.

As we continue our tour, we reach the *Col Saint-Roch*, a pass at an altitude of almost 3,250 ft. near which stands a chapel with a name that seems to be offering an irresistible invitation - Our Lady of Good Nature (*Notre-Dame-de-Bon-Coeur*). It is decorated with a number of works of art including frescoes glorifying the humble everyday work of peasants. At the pass, we shall turn off onto the road to *Lucéram*, once a fortified village as can be seen in the few stretches of crenelated walls and one tower, none of which look particularly recent! Its church (late 15th Century) contains a number of very interesting works of art including the *St. Margaret Reredos* (the predella is in the *Musée Masséna* in Nice) attributed to the great painter

from Nice, *Louis Bréa*, often nicknamed the "*Fra Angelico of Provence*".

From *Lucéram*, you can either head north to *Peïra-Calva*, a winter sports resort and popular summer holiday venue at an altitude of 4,712 ft. then, higher still, the mountain pass (alt. 5,200 ft.) and the magnificent *Turini Forest* which is already part of the *Mercantour National Park*. We shall deal with the park overleaf. For the moment, from *Lucéram*, we shall head back towards Nice via *L'Escarène* (old bridge over the R. Paillon) where there is a very interesting 17th-century *Baroque church*, and the ruins of a *church* that once belonged to the *Order of the Knights Templar*, dating from the 13th Century.

The D 19 forms the north-west exit from Nice. It runs to *Levens*, a pleasant holiday resort from which there is a view of the confluence of the rivers *Var* and *Vésubie*. *Levens* is not only the gateway to the *Vésubie Valley*, justifiably described as one of the most beautiful valleys in the

mountainous hinterland that we are about to visit, but also, if we head slightly further northwards, via the *Mescla Gorge* to the *Tinée Valley.* Although we have passed quickly over these three valleys, they are nevertheless very impressive with their rocks overhanging the road - this no doubt explains the haste with which the road seeks to leave this threatening trap. Not that the lie of the land seems to bother the *River Tinée.* Its peaceful course is far from the tumbling, rumbling mountain stream that one might expect to find in such a spot. It is true that, slightly further upstream, the countryside becomes better-behaved; it is an open, lush valley along which long lines of poplar trees alternate with rows of meadows and perfectly-culti-vated fields. Some twelve miles from the *Mescla Gorge* there is the road junction from which one road leads to *Saint-Sauveur-de-Tinée* and, from there, to distant but famous winter sports resorts such as *Valberg, Auron* or *Isola 2000* while, if you take the D 2565 to the north-east you will reach the *Vésubie Valley.* You will pass *Saint-Martin-de-Vésubie* and arrive very quickly at your destination.

A FOLLOWER OF THE INFAMOUS BLUEBEARD

The route takes us through a strange area that gives its name to a river which visitors arriving from the *Tinée Valley* will be travelling along, but "in the wrong direction" as it were. The name is *Valdeblore.* Having taken the place of the old village of storytellers of old, the "tourist guides" explain that the name (*Valdeblore,* a deformation of *Val des Pleurs,* or Vale of Tears) recalls a legendary figure, the lord of the area who had certain similarities with Bluebeard. He imprisoned an unknown number of wives on whom, and this worsened his case, he imposed what we would now call a "particularly severe diet". In fact, this very unlike-able man left them purely and simply to die of hunger! Hence the name of *Bramafan* (literally, "Calling Hunger") given to the place where their torturer and master kept them prisoner.

Crossed by the waters of the very young *R. Vésubie,* the old town of *Saint-Martin* nestles in the heart of a lush basin, its houses and balconies hanging far out over the river. It gives holidaymakers a wide choice of excursions

Opposite, top:*Saint-Martin-de-Vésubie, a superb beauty spot.*

Opposite, bottom: *A view of the Mercantour National Park (more than 50,000 hectares of unspoiled nature).*

Beyond Saint-Martin-de-Vésubie, Mount Boréon appears in all its splendour.

Saint-Sauveur-sur-Tinée, in Mercantour.

The "Black Virgin" in La Madone de Fenestre.

and walks, through the sumptuous larch forests that grow up to an altitude of 6,500 ft. or along the steep paths on the neighbouring *Boron Range* and, of course, in the beauty spots (covered by protection orders) within the *Mercantour National Park* (53,000 hectares of untamed nature), once the hunting grounds of the Kings of Italy. Another place worth seeing, but further east is the grandiose *Madone de Fenestre* (alt. 6,175 ft.). The chapel is a place of pilgrimage and, in the summer months, it contains a precious cedar-wood statue of the *Black Virgin* said to have been carved by St. Luke himself. In winter, the statue is kept warm in the church in *Saint-Martin*.

In this mountainous region of the *"Azure Alps"*, there is another statue of the Madonna which arouses interest and devotion. This is the *Madonna of Utelle*. To see it, though, we will have to travel down the *R. Vésubie* to *Saint-Julien-la-Rivière*, a village situated 15 miles downstream from *Saint-Martin*. The road is tarmacadamed and open to traffic but it unfurls a series of hairpin bends which are so tight that the patient but powerful Hercules himself would have been totally unable to straighten them out. Once you reach the hamlet of *Utelle*, proud of the feat you have just

Utelle, an observation platform 2,600 feet above the Vésubie.

The hamlet known as "Frenchmen's Leap".

completed, you may, like most visitors, be content with the panoramic view, a splendid sight indeed, from this natural balcony overlooking the valley some 2,600 ft. below. There are those, however, who are more demanding and who will not hesitate to drive round the last few hairpin bends in order to see, in Her sanctuary, the statue of a Madonna which, no doubt to thank them for the fervour that they have shown towards Her, offers the miracle of the most extraordinary, most magnificent, and most beautiful view you could ever dream of. From this isolated peak 3,835 ft. high, the view stretches over the Alps in their ermine white cloak, the mountains of Italy, the vast azure blue of the Mediterranean Sea, the grey or green slopes of Provence, and the red mass of the Estérel Range. Laid out like a map, all the main features can be seen so clearly that the viewing table on the platform is almost useless!

Back in *Saint-Jean-la-Rivière*, we take the D 19 towards *Levens* and, after the terrible hairpin bends leading to *La Madone*, it seems almost like a motorway. Only 3 miles away is an observation platform called "*Le Saut des Français*" ("Frenchmen's Leap"). The curiosity of travellers, though, is quickly satisfied thanks to a commemo-

A bridge in Sospel with an ancient toll tower.

The Madonna of Poggio in Saorge.

rative plaque explaining that this was the spot chosen by the *Barbets* (Royalist rebels from Nice) to throw Republican soldiers who had fallen into their hands down into the abyss. Luckily, this detestable habit seems to have died out these days.

A "MEZZO-MEZZO" RIVER

The *Roya* , which gives its name to the most easterly of the valleys in the hinterland we have been describing, rises and flows through France but, for the last quarter of its course, it resolutely crosses the border and, having become Italian, finally throws itself into the Mediterranean at *Ventimiglia*. During its Italian stage, it is joined by its tributary, the *Bévera*, a river which also rises in France before, in its turn, crossing the border. The *Bévera*, however, flows through *Sospel* so it is this pleasant *alpine resort* that will be the starting-point of a trip which will take us through *Breil-sur-Roya*, the *Saorge Gorge, Saint-Dalmas-de-Tende*, the *Vallée des Merveilles, Notre-Dame-des-Fontaines* and on to *Tendes*.

The "Dark Lake" (Lac Noir) above the Vallée des Merveilles.

The rugged but grandiose landscape in the Bergue Gorge.

Although only just over twelve miles from the coast and lying at an altitude of only 1,138 ft, *Sospel*, for climatic reasons and for its environment of tall mountains with cool streams, fully deserves the description of *alpine resort* which we used before. One of its main sights is an 11th-century bridge on which there is a *Toll Tower*, now perfectly restored and maintained. Note, too, the plaque on the wall of a house adjacent to the church reminding passers-by that Pope Pius VII came here in August 1809 after leaving his *Pontifical States* on the orders of Emperor Napoleon (in this instance, the papal tiara bowed to the will of the bicorn hat).

From *Sospel*, the road passes the *Col de Brouis* (alt. 2,850 ft, superb panoramic view) and runs down to *Breil* and the *Roya Valley*. The road through the *Saorge Gorge* is little more than a narrow cornice slipping through enormous overhanging boulders and it determinedly follows the course of the river, including every twist and turn. Beyond these narrow ravines is another, called the *Bergue Gorge*. Here the rock is flaky red schist, making this an undoubtedly unusual beauty spot. Then comes

Opposite: *A narrow road clinging to the mountainside takes you across the Saorge Gorge.*

Mount Bégo (alt. 9,328 ft) has a number of mysterious "prehistoric" drawings on its slopes.

Saint-Dalmas-de-Tende, the gateway to the famous *Vallée des Merveilles* and the magnificent region dotted with lakes (*Lac du Basto, Lac Noir, Lac Vert, Lac de l'Agnel* etc.) in the shadow of *Mont Bégo* (alt. 9,327 ft.). On its slopes and on the sides of the mountains opposite, are a number of strange drawings, apparently hammered into compact sandstone slabs. There are said to be some 35,000 of them! They represent tools or weapons with mysterious symbols of solar or other significance, "grids", number tables, "cadastral plans" etc. Nobody has ever been able to discover the precise origin of these drawings. They are, though, attributed to "prehistoric men from the lower valleys" (?). One thing that must be said. If you really want to visit the aptly-named *Vallée des Merveilles* fully and in its entirety, it is better to walk along the long-distance waymarked footpaths than remain sitting in your car like those used to main roads and motorways, although the D91 (west of Saint-Dalmas) provides them with resources that are far from negligeable.

THE NIGHTMARE WORK
OF A HALLUCINATED ARTIST

After leaving *Saint-Dalmas* and its pleasant surroundings of chestnut forests, we head for *La Brigue* (eastwards this time) and reach a lost valley crossed by the waters of springs whose rate of flow varies erratically. High above the river is the chapel of *Notre-Dame-des-Fontaines*. From the outside, there is nothing about this very popular place of pilgrimage to give any idea of the incredible treasures contained within, i.e. the admirable frescoes painted by *Jean Canvesio* in the late 15th Century. The composition is marvellous, the colours are rich and perfectly well-preserved, and the frescoes cover the entire walls, running across them like the pages of a strip cartoon. There are twenty-six "rectangles" full of people obviously enjoying the most horrible of practices. As an example, there is a scene representing Judas hanging from the branch of a tree and who, apparently still alive, is looking at his chest which is being ripped

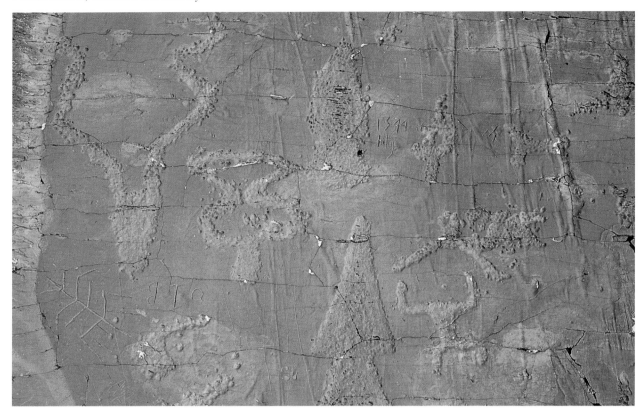

Opposite, top: *Unexplainable messages...*

Opposite, bottom: *the Chapel of Notre-Dame des Fontaines and its admirable paintings.*

Tende where the houses are built in style that might be described as Tibetan!

A hunting scene in La Brigue.

apart by a monster that is a combination of rat and bird of prey. At the same time as his "innards" spill out, a candid cherub with a demon's face is seen rising from the wound. Brrr....! Before undertaking a visit which, although indubitably interesting from an artistic point of view, is also an opportunity to see the forces of Evil being unleashed and which may, therefore, impress certain people by its realism, you will have to stop in *La Brigue* almost 3 miles to the east and fetch the key to the chapel. In any case, *La Brigue* is well worth a visit, if only to admire the houses of black and green schist with their overhanging roofs and the uninterrupted lines of balconies on every floor giving the village a somewhat "Tibetan" atmosphere that is totally unexpected at this latitude.

We will end our tour of the *Upper Roya Valley* at the small town of *Tende*. Like *Saint-Dalmas* and *La Brigue*, *Tende* was annexed to France at the request of its citizens, after a referendum held in 1947.

THE BRAVE "LITTLE TRAIN OF LES PIGNES"

Before ending our description of this superb "ermine white and azure blue" hinterland, we must say just a few words about the vital link between the *"Maritime"* Alps and the Alps in *"Haute Provence"* — the famous Little Train of Les Pignes. It travels from *Nice to Digne* and is

La Bollène-Vésubie.

Opposite: *Black and green schist houses in La Brigue.*

Overleaf: *The "Basto" in the land of frozen lakes, upstream from the Vallée des Merveilles.*

run by the *Chemins de Fer de Provence*. Every day, there are four trains (or five in the summer) between the *prefecture* (county town) of Alpes-Maritimes and the *prefecture* of Alpes-de-Haute-Provence. In order to cover the 93 miles separating these two different worlds, the brave little train has to cross fifteen or more viaducts, twenty-five tunnels (one of which is two miles long), two embankments, and seventeen bridges (the longest is 130 ft.). As it can use the steam locomotive so beloved of our grandparents for part of its journey, the train gives its delighted passengers a chance to enjoy a trip through time and space, thanks to its resolutely anachronistic character. Once it has passed the lower Var Valley, the scenery changes and, through *Villars-sur-Var, Puget-Thénier, Entrevaux* and its *citadel*, there are alternating olive trees, nettle-trees, brambles, poplars, pines, larches, firs etc.

And while the wheels knock against the joins in the rails, making the clink of steel against steel, an equally stubborn stream, rolling against the current, tries, by grinding down the pebbles on its bed, to echo the rumble of the ill-treated metal.

By the time the train arrives in *Annot*, the scenery of Upper Provence has already taken over for a few miles. This is obvious in the *Lac de Castillon*, which appears as the trains exits from the highest tunnel on the line (alt. 3,309 ft.). Then, beyond the pleasant resort of *Saint-André-les-Alpes*, the railway line runs in the same direction as the rivers, all of them flowing westwards towards the *R. Durance*. And when the *Little Train of Les Pignes* finally pulls into Digne Station, out of breath but full of pride, less than three hours have passed since it left the south station in Nice. It is, therefore, quite possible to do a return journey in a day and we wholeheartedly advise readers who are having a holiday on the *Riviera* to leave their car in the garage for a day and really get away from it all!

Région
Provence-Alpes
Côte d'Azur

Briançon

**Hautes-Alpes
05**

GAP

Barcelonnette

Sisteron

**Alpes-de-Haute -
Provence
04**

Vaucluse 84

Carpentras

Forcalquier

DIGNE

**Alpes-Maritimes
06**

AVIGNON

Apt

Manosque

Castellane

MONACO

Grasse

NICE

**PROVENCE-
ALPES-CÔTE D'AZUR**

Arles

Istres

Aix-en-Provence

Draguignan

**Bouches-du-Rhône
13**

Brignoles

**Var
83**

MARSEILLE

TOULON

MER MÉDITERRANÉE

Briançon. The town was given huge fortifications by Vauban in order to block access to the Durance Valley. Nowadays, it is a warm, friendly town with a large hospital and sanitorium.

Digne-les-Bains. Set at an altitude of 1,950 ft. in a circlet of surrounding mountains that protect it from the wind, this is the "Lavender Capital".

Sisteron. Described by Mistral as the "veritable key to Provence", this fine town has an eventful past, as shown in its impressive citadel. This photoshows the Baume Rock.

Aix-en-Provence. Once the "capital" of Provence, Aix is a multi-faceted town with a university, law courts, and spa. It is also famous for its wide-ranging activities in the Arts.

Arles. Nicknamed the "Little Rome of the Gauls" but also the "contented daughter of the Rhône", Arles has developed along each bank of the river that has been its lifeblood, displaying historic buildings that are veritable architectural gems.

Les Baux. This is a unique beauty spot visited over and over again by crowds of tourists who never tire of its proud, rugged beauty!

The Camargue. The light grey horses and black bulls form a striking contrast to the pink wings of the flamingoes, on the shores of reed-lined lakes.

Avignon. Considered, because of its sheer size, as one of the most important historic buildings in the world, the Palace of the Popes serves as a reminder of the prestigious history of this superb Provençal town.

- Digne
- Forcalquier
- Apt
- Vers Sisteron, Gap et Grenoble
- Vers Digne
- Moustiers-Sainte-Marie
- Cas
- Manosque
- ALPES-DE-HAUTE-PROVENCE
- Lac de Sainte-Croix
- Aiguines
- Gorges du Verdon
- C
- sur
- Bauduen
- VAUCLUSE
- Durance
- Saint-Julien-le-Montagné
- Vers Avignon, Valence, Lyon
- Ginasservis
- La Verdière
- Montmeyan
- Aups
- Ampus
- Mo
- Villecroze
- Château
- Varages
- Tavernes
- Sillans-la-Cascade
- Tourtour
- Rians
- Barjols
- Salernes
- Dra
- Aix-en-Provence
- Cotignac
- Entrecasteaux
- Lorgue
- Vers Avignon, Valence, Lyon
- BOUCHES-DU-RHÔNE
- Sources d'Argens
- Montfort-sur-Argens
- Carcès
- V A R
- L
- Argens
- Saint-Maximin-la-Sainte-Baume
- Abbaye de Thoronet
- Vic
- Tourves
- Vers Nîmes et Montpellier
- Rougiers
- Brignoles
- Le Luc-en-Provence
- Saint-Zacharie
- Nans-les-Pins
- Mazaugues
- Besse-sur-Issole
- Le Plan-d'Aups
- La Roquebrussanne
- Gonfaron
- La
- Massif de la Sainte-Baume
- Rocbaron
- Pignans
- Marseille
- Signes
- Méounes
- Notre-Dame-des-Anges
- Massif des
- Aubagne
- Chartreuse de Montrieux
- Cuers
- Chartr de la V
- Pierrefeu-du-Var
- Collobrières
- Le Castellet
- Solliès-Toucas
- La Cadière d'Azur
- Le Beausset
- Solliès-Pont
- Bormes-les-Mimosas
- Cassis
- Solliès-Ville
- C
- Evenos
- Mont Faron
- La Valette
- Le
- La Ciotat
- Saint-Cyr-les-Lecques
- Ollioules
- La Garde
- Bandol
- Le Pradet
- Hyères
- b
- B
- Sanary-sur-Mer
- Toulon
- Brégançon-la-République
- Six-Fours
- La Seyne-sur-Mer
- Carqueiranne
- Le Brusc
- Presqu'île de Giens
- La Tour-Fondue
- Îles d'Hyère
- Porquerolles
- Port

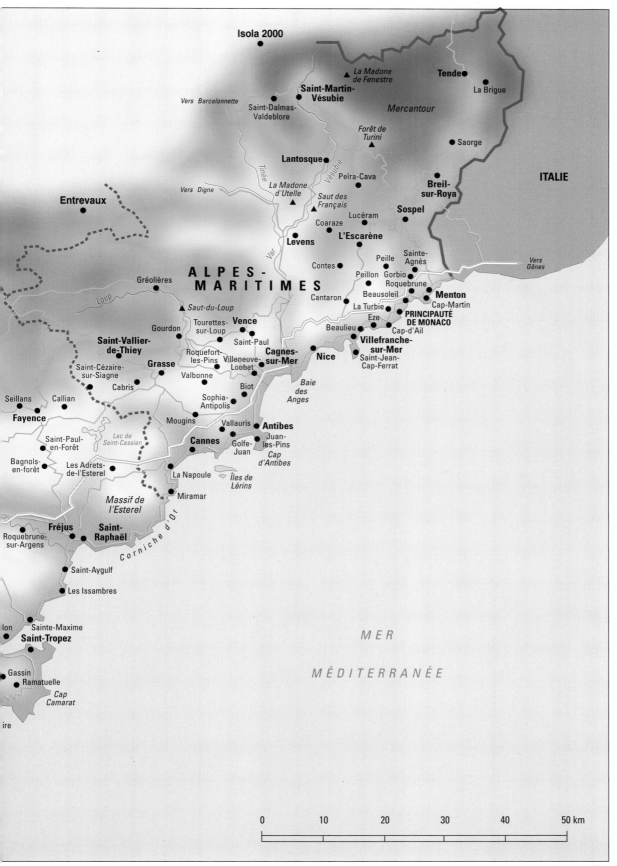

Isola 2000

La Madone
de Fenestre

Tende

La Brigue

Saint-Martin-
Vésubie

Vers Barcelonnette

Saint-Dalmas-
Valdeblore

Mercantour

Forêt de
Turini

Saorge

Lantosque

Vers Digne

La Madone
d'Utelle

Peïra-Cava

Breil-
sur-Roya

ITALIE

Saut des
Français

Lucéram

Sospel

Coaraze

L'Escarène

Levens

Peille

Sainte-
Agnès

Vers
Gênes

ALPES-
MARITIMES

Contes

Peillon

Gorbio

Cantaron

Beausoleil

Roquebrune

Gréolières

Peille

Menton
Cap-Martin

Loup

La Turbie

Saut-du-Loup

Vence

Eze

PRINCIPAUTÉ
DE MONACO

Gourdon

Tourettes-
sur-Loup

Saint-Paul

Beaulieu

Cap-d'Ail

Saint-Vallier-
de-Thiey

Roquefort-
les-Pins

Cagnes-
sur-Mer

Villefranche-
sur-Mer

Nice

Grasse

Villeneuve-
Loubet

Saint-Jean-
Cap-Ferrat

Saint-Cézaire-
sur-Siagne

Valbonne

Cabris

Baie
des
Anges

Seillans

Callian

Sophia-
Antipolis

Biot

Fayence

Mougins

Vallauris

Antibes

Saint-Paul-
en-Forêt

Lac de
Saint-Cassien

Cannes

Golfe-
Juan

Juan-
les-Pins

Bagnols-
en-forêt

Cap
d'Antibes

Les Adrets-
de-l'Esterel

La Napoule

Îles de
Lérins

Miramar

Massif de
l'Esterel

Corniche d'Or

Fréjus

Saint-
Raphaël

Roquebrune-
sur-Argens

Saint-Aygulf

Les Issambres

MER

Ion

Sainte-Maxime

Saint-Tropez

MÉDITERRANÉE

Gassin
Ramatuelle

Cap
Camarat

ire

0   10   20   30   40   50 km

Cartography :
P. Rekacewicz.

TABLE OF CONTENTS

Soft back:
Front cover: VILLEFRANCHE.

Back cover: UTELLE.

Hard back:
Front cover: CAP MARTIN.

Back cover: PEILLE.

Cet ouvrage a été achevé d'imprimer par Pollina, 85400 luçon - n° 73610
I.S.B.N. 2.7373.1724.X - Dépôt légal : février 1995
N° d'éditeur : 3145.03.03.01.98